The **SUNDAY TIMES** Book of
Garden Quotations

Graham Rose & Peter King

With an Introduction by
Victoria Glendinning

QUARTET
LONDON   MELBOURNE   NEW YORK

First published by
Quartet Books Limited
in association with the *Sunday Times* 1986
A member of the Namara Group
27/29 Goodge Street
London W1P 1FD

British Library Cataloguing in Publication Data

Green Words: the Sunday Times book of garden
    quotations
    1. Gardening – Quotations, maxims, etc.
    I. Rose, Graham   II. King, Peter, 1925
    635   SB455

ISBN 0–7043–2590–X

Designed by Namara Design
Typeset by M.C. Typeset, Chatham, Kent
Printed and bound in Great Britain by
Nene Litho and Woolnough Bookbinding
both of Wellingborough, Northants

> The garden was a wide enclosure, sur-
> rounded with walls so high as to exclude
> every glimpse of prospect; a covered veran-
> dah ran down one side, and broad walks
> bordered a middle space divided into scores
> of little beds: these beds were assigned as
> gardens for the pupils to cultivate, and each
> bed had an owner. When full of flowers they
> would doubtless look pretty.

CHARLOTTE BRONTË, *Jane Eyre*

On 10 November 1985 the *Sunday Times* Colour Magazine published this quotation from Charlotte Brontë's *Jane Eyre* which had won a competition inviting readers to select the best passage about gardens which they could discover in literature. Both literary merit and the possibility of reproducing the garden described as the *Sunday Times* exhibit at the Chelsea Flower Show were considered by the judges. The quotation subsequently became the subject of a design competition to choose the best interpretation of Charlotte Brontë's words from which to build the garden at Chelsea. Along with their quotations many contestants sent notes saying that they would welcome the publication of a selection of the best quotes submitted.

For some years biographer and playwright Peter King and *Sunday Times* gardening correspondent Graham Rose had been collecting quotations with gardens or features in gardens as their theme. A careful selection and editing of both collections by Peter King lead to the compilation of *Green Words*, in which Graham Rose comments on the relevance of the garden designs or features to gardeners today.

Contents

Acknowledgements

In compiling any anthology, one not only has the help of all the authors from whose work prose or verse has been chosen, but also from other anthologists. Of the latter, the works of Edith Sitwell, the Hadfields and Julia S. Berrall are particularly to be mentioned. Thanks are also due to entrants in the *Sunday Times* Literary Garden Competition who so diligently searched their libraries and bookshelves for good garden quotes, many of which appear in this collection. We regret that all the quotes submitted could not be included and that those who sent in quotes could not be acknowledged personally. The editors are much obliged also to those friends who suggested quotations for inclusion in the anthology, and particularly to William Husselby for his help.

We are also very grateful to the *Sunday Times*, without whose co-operation this book would not have been possible.

All extracts have been reproduced, as far as possible, in the style in which they appeared originally, although some spellings have been modernized for the sake of readability.

Every effort has been made to contact copyright holders; the editors apologize for any inadvertent omissions. For permission to reprint material in this anthology acknowledgement is made as follows: E.M. Forster for an extract from *A Room with a View*, to Edward Arnold (Publishers) Ltd; E. Nisbet for an extract from *Long Ago when I was Young* to Macdonald and Co (Publishers) Ltd; Harold Nicolson for the letter from his diaries, to Collins Publishers; F. Scott Fitzgerald for two extracts from

The Bodley Head Scott Fitzgerald Vol. I, to The Bodley Head Ltd; P.G. Wodehouse for an extract from *Thank You Jeeves*, to the Trustees of the Wodehouse Trust no. 3 and Century Hutch-inson Ltd; Virginia Woolf for two extracts from *Between the Acts* and *The Waves*, to the author's estate and the Hogarth Press.

The illustrations are taken from *Garden Architecture A Pictorial Guide for Gardens Old and New* which was kindly provided by Sonia Ewart.

Introduction

Most of the garden books on our shelves are practical, and we read them to check out what to plant and where, how to propagate and how to plan. With a few famous exceptions, we do not read them as literature. Many of the passages of prose and poetry in this book were among the hundreds sent in by those readers of the *Sunday Times* who entered the Literary Garden Competition in 1985; others have been collected over the years by Graham Rose and Peter King. They have avoided professional gardening writers, even the best ones; the gardens in this book, real or imaginary, are evoked by poets, letter-writers, memoirists, novelists. But a practical gardener cannot resist visualizing a garden which is described in words, however poetic or impressionistic the words may be. Graham Rose accepts the challenge and provides suggestions about how types of garden, or garden features, may be realized or re-created.

All gardening and garden planning means hard work. Even poets – some of them – know that. Rudyard Kipling, himself a dedicated gardener, wrote that

> . . . gardens are not made
> By singing 'Oh how beautiful!' and sitting in the shade,
> While better men than we go out and start their working
>   lives
> At grubbing weeds from gravel paths with broken
>   dinner-knives.

Kipling was thinking of garden-boys, apprenticed to a head gardener. Nowadays people grub the weeds from gravel paths themselves, or treat them with weedkiller. But there are indeed better ways of appreciating a garden than singing 'Oh how beautiful!' A few of the gardens conjured up in these pages may not seem beautiful at all, or not to everyone. Why do some garden designs and some planting schemes please us, and others not? The packed displays in formally planted and colourful borders which are the pride of one may strike horror into the heart of another who prefers architectural plant groupings in austere tones of green and grey. Pride and prejudice haunt the garden, as most others areas of life.

This anthology is an appeal to the seeing eye, the musical ear and the open mind. There are authors represented here whom we might never normally come across. There are descriptions in widely diverse forms and styles of every kind of garden from ancient times to our own, by writers with the skill to evoke atmosphere in words far more telling than 'Oh how beautiful!'

Some of these gardens are fantastical, some have their structure soberly documented, some are simple, some elaborate. There are lavish, busy gardens, and others so formal in terms of linear design, stone and statuary, that plant life seems to be there on sufferance, standing to order like clipped poodles at a dog show. There are many which owe their existence on the printed page in the first place to some purely human drama which is the writer's chief concern.

Charlotte Brontë in *Jane Eyre* was more interested in her heroine's unacknowledged passion for her employer than in the scented garden where his cigar glowed in the dark. In an even more famous literary garden, Tennyson was keener on luring Maud out of doors than in the passion-flower at the gate. Yet the human emotions intensify these visions of gardens – which are always, in any case, sexy places. For that, we have to thank Adam and Eve, who discovered what life was about in the first garden, the Garden of Eden.

Gardens can also be sinister – not by night only, but in brilliant sunlight. Elizabeth Bowen, in a short story, describes a couple, lost on the road, approaching a strange house to ask their way: 'Each side of the path, hundreds of standard roses bloomed, overcharged with colour, as if this were their one hour. Crimson, coral, blue-pink, lemon and cold white, they disturbed with fragrance the dead air.' The roses 'glared at the strangers, frighteningly bright'. The place was 'a trap baited with beauty'. I would not want to advance between those menacing ranks of roses.

The most surprising authors fill their books with gardens. We think of H.G. Wells as an early science-fiction writer; and later, he produced a spate of novels preaching his doctrines of free love and a World State. But these didactic fictions are crammed with descriptions of gardens. Most of them are in Surrey, backing on to pine woods, and sound as if they were designed by Gertrude Jekyll. Here is a corner of one of them:

> There was a rose garden all blooming in chorus, and with pillar-roses and arches that were not so much growths as overflowing cornucopias of roses, and a neat orchard with shapely trees white-painted to their exact middles, a stone wall bearing clematis and a clothesline so gay with Mr Brumley's blue and white flannel shirts that it seemed an essential part of the design.

That garden, wrote Wells, was 'full of things that people dream about doing in their gardens and mostly never do'. This anthology, we think, will enable readers not only to dream other people's garden dreams, and their own, but to set to work and make sure they come true. The word 'Paradise' simply means an enclosure; it is a private space where we come to grips with nature as nowhere else, though not always successfully: even that great gardener V. Sackville-West used to say *'Beastly garden!'* when nature was getting the upper hand.

But I am writing in February – a singularly dark, dismal, sleety February. Both nature and I are observing a truce, so far as I can tell. Neither of us is doing a lot, and Paradise must be in another country. I presume nature is up to something: the snowdrops are out, *Daphne mezereum* is swelling interestingly, winter jasmine is over. But the *Clematis montana* which is meant to smother the shed has escaped from its moorings on the roof and is flopping down like a slipped wig. The dog, frustrated in her career as an escapologist by the new panel fencing with trellis top, has dug two massive holes in the lawn. There are puzzling empty spaces in the icy beds: did I plant tulips there? Did I redistribute herbaceous plants badly in the autumn? Has something surreptitiously died? It is time to turn to other writers' *Green Words* for inspiration, since there is none in the view from my windows.

Gardening is obsessional; it can keep you awake at night, planning and visualizing. This anthology, while not robbing you of your preoccupation, may soothe the savage breast. More importantly, it will keep you out of the garden when the day's work and pleasure are over. It is important to control gardener's twitch – the impulse that drives one out, possibly for the fifth time, on a summer evening, to mooch around fussily yet again . . . and yet again, first thing in the morning, noting changes the night has brought, brooding over stubborn buds, crouching over cuttings, flicking at them to see if they have taken, gazing reproachfully at the new shrub that promised so much but is delivering so little.

Plants don't like to be stared at too much while they are doing what they have to do. Science, or para-science, tells us that geraniums bloom better if they are spoken to. But a kind word every now and then is really quite enough. Too much attention, like too much feeding and weeding and hoeing, inhibits and embarrasses them. One of my own favourite garden quotations is not a description of a garden but a recommendation to leave the poor garden alone. Again it is from H.G. Wells: 'A garden, even when it is not exasperated by intensive methods, is a thing as exacting as a baby . . . Intensive cultivation greatly increases this disposition to trouble mankind; it makes a garden touchy and hysterical, a drugged and demoralized and over-irritated garden.'

So for your own and your garden's sake, put your feet up and enjoy *Green Words*.

VICTORIA GLENDINNING

Temples and
Arbours

AN ANCIENT WILL AND A TEMPLE

I give to Callinus the land which I possess at Stagira, and all my books to Neleus. As to my garden, the walk, and the houses adjacent to the garden, I give them in perpetuity to those of my friends mentioned below, who desire to devote themselves in common to study and philosophy therein, for everyone cannot always travel: provided that they shall not be able to alienate this property; it shall not belong to any of them individually, but they shall own it in common as a sacred possession, and shall enjoy it peaceably and amicably as it is just and fitting. I admit to this common enjoyment Hipparchus, Neleus, Straton, Callinus, Demotimus, Democrates, Callisthenes, Melanthus, Pancreon, and Nicippus. Aristotle, son of Metrodorus and of Pythias, shall enjoy the same rights, and shall share them with these, if he desires to devote himself to philosophy; in this case, the eldest shall take every possible care of him, to the end that he may make progress in science. I desire to be buried in the part of the garden judged to be most fitting, and no excessive expense shall be incurred for my funeral or my tomb. After the last rites have been paid me according to my will, and the temple, my tomb, my garden, and the walk have been provided for, I direct that Pompylus, who inhabits the garden, shall keep the custody of it, as before, and that he shall likewise have the superintendence of all the rest.

THEOPHRASTUS

THE ARBOUR

And shapen was this herber, roofe and all,
As is a pretty parlour; and also
The hegge as thicke as is a castle wall,
So that who list withoute to stand or go,

Though he would all day prien to and fro,
He shoulde not see if there were any wighte
Within or no; but one within well mighte
Perceive alle that yeden there withoute.

GEOFFREY CHAUCER

A STATELY ARCHED HEDGE

The garden is best to be square; encompassed, on all
the four sides, with a stately arched hedge. The arches
to be upon pillars of carpenter's work, of some ten foot
high and six foot broad; and the spaces between of the
same dimension with the breadth of the arch. Over the
arches let there be an entire hedge, of some four foot
high, framed also upon carpenter's work; and upon the
upper hedge, over every arch, a little turret, with a belly,
enough to receive a cage of birds; and over every space
between the arches some other little figure, with broad
plates of round coloured glass, gilt, for the sun to play
upon. But this hedge I intend to be raised upon a bank,
not steep, but gently slope, of some six foot, set all with
flowers. Also I understand that this square of the garden
should not be the whole breadth of the ground, but to
leave, on either side, ground enough for diversity of side
alleys; unto which the two covert alleys of the green may
deliver you. But there must be no alleys with hedges at

either end of this great enclosure: not at the hither end, for letting your prospect upon this fair hedge from the green; nor at the further end, for letting your prospect from the hedge, through the arches, upon the heath.

FRANCIS BACON

A USEFUL DOME

Now bricklay'rs, carpenters and joiners,
With Chinese artists and designers
Produce their schemes of alteration
To work this wond'rous reformation.
The useful dome, which secret stood
Embosom'd in the yew-tree's wood,
The trav'ler with amazement sees
A temple, Gothic or Chinese,
With many a bell, and tawdry rag on
And crested with a sprawling dragon;

ROBERT LLOYD

OF TRELLIS VINES

Methought I stood where trees of every clime,
Palm, myrtle, oak, and sycamore, and beech,
With plantain, and spice-blossoms, made a screen;
In neighbourhood of fountains (by the noise
Soft-showering in my ears), and, (by the touch
Of scent) not far from roses. Turning round
I saw an arbour with a drooping roof
Of trellis vines, and bells, and larger blooms,
Like floral censers, swinging light in air;

JOHN KEATS

SWEET RETREAT

There was a bower at the further end, with honeysuckle, jessamine, and creeping plants—one of those sweet retreats which humane men erect for spiders.

The spinster aunt took up a large watering-pot which lay in one corner, and was about to leave the arbour. Mr Tupman detained her, and drew her to a seat beside him.

'Miss Wardle!' said he.

The spinster aunt trembled, till some pebbles which had accidentally found their way into the large watering-pot shook like an infant's rattle.

'Miss Wardle,' said Mr Tupman, 'you are an angel.'

'Mr Tupman!' exclaimed Rachael, blushing as red as the watering-pot itself.

'Nay,' said the eloquent Pickwickian—'I know it but too well.'

'All women are angels, they say,' murmured the lady, playfully.

'Then what can *you* be; or to what, without presumption, can I compare you?' replied Mr Tupman. 'Where was the woman ever seen, who resembled you? Where else could I hope to find so rare a combination of excellence and beauty? Where else could I seek to—Oh!' Here Mr Tupman paused, and pressed the hand which clasped the handle of the happy watering-pot.

CHARLES DICKENS

THE MASTER WORK-MAN'S BOW'R

'Twas bench'd with Turf, and goodly to be seen,
The thick young Grass arose in fresher Green:
The Mound was newly made, no Sight cou'd pass
Betwixt the nice Partitions of the Grass;
The well-united Sods so closely lay;
And all arround the Shades defended it from Day.
For Sycamours with Eglantine were spread,
A Hedge about the Sides, a Covering over Head.
And so the fragrant Briar was wove between,
The Sycamour and Flow'rs were mix'd with Green,
That Nature seem'd to vary the Delight;
And satisfy'd at once the Smell and Sight.
The Master Work-man of the Bow'r was known
Through Fairy-Lands, and built for *Oberon*:
Who twining Leaves with such Proportion drew,
They rose by Measure, and by Rule they grew:
No mortal Tongue can half the Beauty tell,
For none but Hands divine could work so well,
Both Roof and Sides were like a Parlour made,
A soft Recess, and a cool Summer Shade;
The Hedge was set so thick, no Foreign Eye
The Persons plac'd within it could espy;

JOHN DRYDEN

WALKS

The Ancients used to make their Walks into a Kind of
Arbours by Means of Vines supported by Columns of
Marble of the Corinthian Order, which were ten of their
own Diameters in Height. The Trees ought to be
planted in Rows exactly even, and answering to one

another exactly upon straight Lines: and the Gardens should be enriched with rare Plants, and such are in most Esteem among the Physicians. It was a good agreeable Piece of Flattery among the ancient Gardeners, to trace their Masters Names in Box, or in sweet-smelling Herbs, in Parterres.

SCIPIONE ALBERTI

AMARYLLIS AT THE ARBOUR

One side of the summer-house was a thick holly-bush. Iden had set it there; he builded the summer-house and set the ivy; and the pippin at the back, whose bloom was white, the copper-beech nearby; the great sycamore alone had been there before him, but he set a seat under it, and got woodbine to flower there; the drooping ash he planted, and if Amaryllis stood under it when the tree was in full leaf you could not see her, it made so complete an arbour; the Spanish oak in the corner; the box hedge along the ha-ha carpet; the red currants against the red wall; the big peony yonder; the damsons and pear; the yellow honeybush; all these, and this was but one square, one mosaic of the garden, half of it sward, too, and besides these there was the rhubarb-patch at one corner; fruit, flowers, plants and herbs, lavender, parsley, which has a very pleasant green, growing in a thick bunch, roses, pale sage.

RICHARD JEFFERIES

TEMPLES AND ARBOURS

No one who can afford it need be deprived of a temple in his or her garden. But the cost can run to several hundred or even thousands of pounds. And usually, unless the rest of the garden is very grand, such features tend to look absurd. In an unpretentious garden, it is probably better to have a simple design of iron frame made up by a local blacksmith, or to build a timber and iron temple yourself.

One of the easiest ways to make an attractive arbour is to follow the example of our Victorian ancestors. They instructed their blacksmiths to make them a bee-hive-shaped framework from iron rod some eight to ten feet high at the top of the dome with a circular base of approximately eight feet in diameter. An arched entrance to the structure six feet high and thirty inches wide was formed in the side of the dome which was left uncovered when the rest of the dome was clad in chicken wire. Ivy or other evergreen climbers planted round the perimeter of the dome base soon scrambled all over its wire cladding and created a charming leafy arbour inside the dome which offered shade in sunny weather and infinite possibilities for the exchange of intimacies.

G.R.

Statues, Ruins and Grottos

BOBOLI GARDENS

There were no gardens there like those
That, groomed for pleasure and for ease,
Rose-clouded with the laurel-rose,
Hung high above blue distances.

There were no fountains, dolphin-fed
For idle eyes to drift upon,
Where gold-fish, flecking green with red,
Drift idle in the eternal sun;

No sloping alleys gliding smooth
Through velvet glooms or golden light,
Round-moulded like the marble youth
That stops the alley-way with white;

No naiad . . .

EDMUND WILSON

OF GARDENS

So I have made a platform of a princely garden, partly by
precept, partly by drawing—not a model, but some
general lines of it—and in this I have spared for no cost;
but it is nothing for great princes, that, for the most part,
taking advice with workmen, with no less cost, set their
things together, and sometimes add statues, and such
things, for state and magnificence, but nothing to the
true pleasure of a garden.

FRANCIS BACON

STATUES THAT SEEM TO BREATHE

Nonsuch, a royal retreat, in a place formerly called
Cuddington, a very healthful situation, chosen by King
Henry VIII for his pleasure and retirement, and built by
him with an excess of magnificence and elegance, even
to ostentation; one would imagine everything that
architecture can perform, to have been employed in this
one work: there are everywhere so many statues, that
seem to breathe, so many miracles of consummate art,
so many charts that rival even the perfecting of Roman
antiquity, that it may well claim and justify its name of
Nonsuch, being without an equal, as the poet sung:

This which no equal has in art or fame,
Britons deservedly do Nonsuch name.

PAUL HENTZNER

Besides two galleries and a circular portico filled with
antique statues, there are pieces of sculpture of every
description scattered about the gardens: caryatides,
torsos, colossal busts, gods, columns topped with busts,
urns, lions, huge vases, pedestals, and their innumerable remains, often broken or mutilated. In order to
turn everything to account, a wall is frequently en-
crusted with quantities of shapeless fragments. Some of
these sculptures, such as caryatides, a mask of Antinous,
and certain statues of emperors are fine; but the greater
part forms a singular collection. Many of them be-
longed, evidently, to small municipalities and private
dwellings; they are workshop stock, already familiar to
the ancients, and the same as would subsist with us, if
after a long period of inhumation our stairway statues

and *hotel de ville* busts should be discovered; they may be regarded as museum documents rather than as works of art.

HENRI TAINE

Statues and vases contribute very much to the embellishment and magnificence of a garden, and extremely advance the natural beauties of it. They are made of several forms, and different materials; the richest of those are cast-brass, lead gilt, and marble; the ordinary sort are of common stone, or stucco. Among figures are distinguish'd groups, which consist of at least two figures together in the same block; figures insulate, or detached, that is, those you can go quite round; and figures that are set in niches, which are finish'd on the fore-part only.

There are likewise, busts, terms, half-length figures; figures half as big as the life, and those bigger than the life, called *Colossal*, placed either on regular pedestals, or such as are more slender, tapering and hollowed, or on flat plinths; not to mention the figures of animals, which sometimes adorn cascades; as do brass-relievos and mask-heads.

A.J.D. D'ARGENVILLE

FIT ONLY FOR PRINCES

These figures represent all the several deities, and illustrious persons of antiquity, which should be placed properly in gardens, setting the river gods, as the *Naiades, Rivers*, and *Tritons*, in the middle of fountains and basons; and those of the woods, as *Sylvanes, Faunes,* and *Dryads* in the groves: sacrifices, bacchanals, and children's sports, are likewise represented in bass-relieve, upon the vases and pedestals, which may be adorn'd with festoons, foliage, moldings, and other ornaments.

The usual places of figures and vases are along the palisades, in the front, and upon the sides of a parterre; in the niches and sinkings of hornbeam, or of lattice-work made for that purpose. In groves, they are placed in the centre of a star, or *S. Andrew's* Cross; in the spaces between the walks of a goose-foot, in the middle of halls and cabinets, among the trees and arches of a green-gallery, and at the head of a row of trees, or palisades, that stand free and detached. They are also put at the lower end of walks and vistas, to set them off the better; in porticos, and arbors of trellis-work; in basons, cascades, &c.

In general, they do well everywhere; and you can scarce have too many of them in a garden: but, as in the business of sculpture, it should be excellent, as well as in paintings and poesy (which are its two sisters). I think it more advisable for a private gentleman to be content without figures, than to take up with such as are but indifferent, which do but create a continual longing after this perfection; the expense of which is fit only for princes, and great ministers.

A.J.D. D'ARGENVILLE

POPE'S GROTTO – VERY POETICAL

You shew yourself a just man and a friend in those guesses and suppositions you make at the possible reasons of my silence; every one of which is a true one. As to forgetfulness of you and yours, I assure you, the promiscuous conversations of the town serve only to put me in mind of better, and more quiet, to be had in a corner of the world (undisturbed, innocent, serene, and sensible) with such as you. Let no access of any distrust make you think of me differently in a cloudy day from what you do in the most sunshiny weather. Let the young ladies be assured I make nothing new in my gardens without wishing to see the print of their fairy steps in every part of them. I have put the last hand to my works of this kind, in happily finishing the subter- raneous way and grotto. I there found a spring of the clearest water, which falls in a perpetual rill, that echoes through the cavern day and night. From the river Thames, you see through my arch up a walk of the wilderness, to a kind of open temple, wholly composed of shells in the rustic manner; and from that distance under the temple you look down through a sloping arcade of trees, and see the sails on the river passing suddenly and vanishing, as through a perspective glass. When you shut the doors of this grotto, it becomes on the instant, from a luminous room, a *camera obscura*; on the walls of which all the objects of the river, hills, wood, and boats, are forming a moving picture in their visible radiations: And when you have a mind to light it up, it affords you a very different scene. It is finished with shells interspersed with pieces of looking-glass in angular forms; and in the ceiling is a star of the same material, at which when a lamp (of an orbicular figure of thin alabaster).is hung in the middle, a thousand pointed rays glitter, and are reflected over the place. There are connected to this grotto by a narrower passage two porches, one towards the river of smooth stones full of light, and open; the other toward the garden shadowed with trees, rough with shells, flints, and iron ore. The bottom is paved with simple pebble, as is also the adjoining walk up the wilderness to the temple, in the natural taste, agreeing not ill with the little dripping murmur, and the aquatic idea of the whole place. It wants nothing to complete it but a good statue with an inscription, like that beautiful antique one which you know I am so fond of,

Hujus Nympha loci, sacri custodia fontis,
Dormio, dum blande sentio murmur aque.
Parce meum, quisquis tangis cava marmora, somnum
Rupere; si bibas, sive lavere, tace.

Nymph of the grot, these sacred springs I keep,
And to the murmur of these waters sleep;
Ah spare my slumbers gently tread the cave!
And drink in silence, or in silence lave!

You will think I have been very poetical in this description, but it is pretty near the truth. I wish you were here to bear testimony how little it owes to art, either the place itself, or the image I give of it.

ALEXANDER POPE

POPE'S GROTTO – PROSAIC

Being under the necessity of making a subterraneous passage to a garden on the other side of the road, he adorned it with fossile bodies, and dignified it with the title of a grotto; a place of silence and retreat, from which he endeavoured to persuade his friends and himself that cares and passions could be excluded.

A grotto is not often the wish or pleasure of an Englishman, who has more frequent need to solicit than exclude the sun; but Pope's excavation was requisite as an entrance to his garden, and, as some men try to be proud of their defects, he extracted an ornament from an inconvenience, and vanity produced a grotto where necessity enforced a passage.

SAMUEL JOHNSON

ON HIS GROTTO AT TWICKENHAM COMPOSED OF MARBLES, SPARS, GEMS, ORES AND MINERALS

Thou who shall stop, where Thames' translucent Wave
Shines a broad Mirrour thro' the shadowy Cave;
Where lingering Drops from Mineral Roofs distil,
And pointed Crystals break the sparkling Rill,
Unpolish'd Gemms no Ray on Pride bestow,
And latent Metals innocently glow:
Approach. Great Nature studiously behold!
An eye the Mine without a Wish for Gold.
Approach: but awful! Lo th' Aegerian Grott,
Where, nobly-pensive, St John sate and thought;
Where British Sighs from dying Wyndham stole,
And the bright Flame was shot thro' Marchmont's Soul.
Let such, such only, tread this sacred Floor,
Who dare to love their Country, and be poor.

ALEXANDER POPE

A SUNG GROTTO

On the West, a walk through weeping willows leads to the bank of the river. All around are rocks piled casually with an effect like that of an amphitheatre. At the base is the entrance to a grotto, which as one goes in, gets wider, making an irregularly-shaped room with an arched ceiling. Light comes from above through an opening hung around with wild vines and honeysuckle. Rocks serve as seats and here on the blazing dog days one can sit in the cool shadowy cave, refreshed by the sight and sound of water, for a small stream comes out on one side and fills the hollow of a great stone, and then trickles to the floor, winding about in cracks and fissures till it falls into an open basin. The basin becomes deeper, turns, and flows into a pond at the bottom of the grotto, leaving space for a little path which wanders between the water and the great natural-shaped rocks which are heaped around. A whole family of rabbits plays around the rocks and fishes dart to and fro in the pond . . .

HSI MA-KUANG

A PERSIAN GROTTO

In the centre of these shady labyrinths, stands a kind of grotto or temple, which, from its construction, materials, and distribution of water, must, in summer, be delightful from its coolness and seclusion. Few of the flowers were in bud, when I first visited this charming spot; but the balmy season, advancing with singular rapidity in these high tracts of Persia, soon covered

every mountain's brow with rich herbage, and filled the
whole air with perfume from the full-blown gardens . . .

SIR ROBERT KER PORTER

DEEP IN A DARKSOME GROVE

Deep in a darksome grove their Grotto lies,
And deep the thoughts that now within me rise.
Fronting the door the South Hill looming near,
The forest mirrored in the river clear,
The bamboo bends beneath last winter's snow,
The court-yard darkens ere the day sinks low.
I seem to pass beyond this world of clay,
And sit and listen to the spring-birds' lay.

TSU YUNG

A NUDE CHILD WITH TUMMY

The sun was shining. The sky was blue – and London
seemed miles away – which it was, of course. I wouldn't
be exaggerating if I said that a great peace enveloped the
soul.

A thing I never know when I'm telling a story is how
much scenery to bung in. I've asked one or two
scriveners of my acquaintance, and their views differ. A
fellow I met at a cocktail party in Bloomsbury said that
he was all for describing kitchen sinks and frowsty
bedrooms, and squalor generally, but the beauties of
Nature, no. Whereas Freddie Oaker, of the Drones,
who does tales of pure love for the weeklies under the
pen-name of Alicia Seymour, once told me that he

reckoned that flowery meadows in springtime alone
were worth at least a hundred quid a year to him.

Personally, I've always rather barred long descriptions of the terrain, so I will be on the brief side. As I
stood there that morning, what the eye rested on was the
following. There was a nice little splash of garden,
containing a bush, a tree, a couple of flower beds, a lily
pond with a statue of a nude child with a bit of a tummy
on him, and to the right a hedge . . . There was another
hedge straight ahead, with the garden gate in it, and
over this one espied the placid waters of the harbour,
which was much about the same as any other harbour.

P.G. WODEHOUSE

APRÈS TROIS ANS

Ayant poussé la porte étroite qui chancelle,
Je me suis promené dans le petit jardin
Qu'éclairait doucement le soleil du matin,
Pailletant chaque fleur d'une humide étincelle.

Rien n'a changé. J'ai tout revu: l'humble tonnelle
De vigne folle avec les chaises de rotin . . .
Le jet d'eau fait toujours son murmure argentin
Et le vieux tremble sa plainte sempiternelle.

Les roses comme avant palpitent; comme avant,
Les grands lys orgueilleux se balancent au vent.
Chaque alouette qui va et vient m'est connue.

Même j'ai retrouvé debout la Velléda,*

Dont le plâtre s'écaille au bout de l'avenue,
– Grêle, parmi l'odeur fade du réséda.

PAUL VERLAINE

*Her statue is in the Luxembourg Gardens, Paris

CALYPSO'S CAVE OR GROTTO

The cave was sheltered by a verdant copse of alders, aspens, and fragrant cypresses, which was the roosting-place of feathered creatures, horned owls and falcons and garrulous choughs, birds of the coast, whose daily business takes them down to the sea. Trailing round the very mouth of the cavern, a garden vine ran riot, with great bunches of ripe grapes; while from four separate but neighbouring springs four crystal rivulets were trained to run this way and that; and in soft meadows on either side the iris and the parsley flourished.

HOMER

STATUES

Imagine yourself a Medici prince who, walking in his garden at Boboli, could not help seeing the city of Florence in the distance (as we still can today). Florence, that hotbed of political intrigue, was not a restful sight for a Medici, and so he needed focal points inside the garden on which his eye might rest. You would not expect to find Edmund Wilson in Italy; the American writer was more at home in the Algonquin Hotel lounge producing something for the next issue of *New Yorker* magazine. His writing usually has a harsh tone, both in his novels and in his critical and political writing, but here it is clear that there was a softer edge to his nature, almost romantic, but with the critical awareness to see that statuary's main role in a garden is not to decorate, but to provide such focal points.

Genuine statuary, or its cheaper substitutes, sundials, birdbaths and benches, are probably more important in small gardens than in the environs of the palace, because buildings seen from the small garden may be offensive. But garden designers must be careful not to make the distracting statue more obtrusive than the eyesore – it must beckon invitingly but not scream. Its colour and texture must contrast sufficiently with that of its background to make it clearly seen, but it must harmonize rather than clash with its surroundings, and this balance can be hard to achieve.

Even more important is the question of scale. The giant vases, urns, and classical figures of the eighteenth century, provide focal points for vistas measured in kilometres, but they would look totally absurd in smaller gardens, making the area look mean and cramped (this has happened in a good many public parks). Most designers strive to make small gardens deceptively large and this can be accomplished only if the artefacts are of an appropriate scale. Fortunately, after years of appearing to ignore small gardeners, sculptors, masons and potters seem to have begun at last to appreciate their needs. A hunt round the garden centres, potteries and craft centres should produce a range of reasonably priced objects which would look well and make good focal points. One often neglected source is the sculpture studios of our art schools where a donation is always appreciated, and its bestowal generates a warming sense of patronage. And who knows but that the student sculptor today may ultimately turn out to have been an embryo Michelangelo or Moore?

One error to be avoided when choosing artefacts for the garden is to select something out of character – either with the garden or the region. Nothing looks more pompous and out-of-place than classical marble in what is essentially a 'cottagy' type of garden. Something carved in wood might be better, or fragments of broken stone clad in ivy or allowed to become moss-covered. And those who put pretentious heraldic animals on the garden gates rarely hit quite the note they intended.

G.R.

Seats, Steps and Terraces

A SEAT TO SUP UPON

At the upper end is a semicircular bench of white
marble, shaded with a vine which is trained upon four
small pillars of Carystian marble. Water, gushing
through several little pipes from under this bench, as if
it were pressed out by the weight of the persons who
repose themselves upon it, falls into a stone cistern
underneath, from whence it is received into a fine
polished marble basin, so artfully contrived that it is
always full without ever overflowing. When I sup here,
the tray of whets and the larger dishes are placed
around the margin, while the smaller ones swim about
in the form of little ships and waterfowl. Opposite this is
a fountain which is incessantly emptying and filling, for
the water which it throws up to a great height falling
back again into it, is by means of connected openings
returned as fast as it is received.

PLINY

BAROQUE STEPS

In the centre of the courtyard, to the left of stables and
riding-school, stood two high pillars in porous yellow
stone, adorned with masks and scrolls, which opened on
to a flight of steps leading down into the garden. They
were a short flight (a dozen or so steps in all) but in that
space the baroque architect had found ways of expressing a freakish and whimsical turn of mind, alternating
high and low steps, twisting motifs together in most
unexpected ways, creating superfluous little landings
with niches and benches so as to produce in this small
space a variety of possible joinings and separations, of

brusque rejections and affectionate reconciliations, which imparted to the staircase the atmosphere of a lovers' tiff.

GIUSEPPE DI LAMPEDUSA

BENCHES

My gardens sweet, enclosed with walles strong,
  Embanked with benches to sitt and take my rest
  The knotts so enknotted it cannot be exprest
With arbours and alyes so pleasant and dulce
The pestilent ayers with flavors to repulse.

GEORGE CAVENDISH

POPE ON SHERBORNE

You come first out of the house into a green walk of standard limes with a hedge behind them that makes a colonnade, thence into a little triangular wilderness, from whose centre you see the town of Sherborne in a valley, interspersed with trees.

From the corner of this you issue at once upon a high grown terrace the whole breadth of the garden, which has five more green terraces hanging one under another, without hedges, only a few pyramid yews and large round honeysuckles between them. The honey-suckles hereabouts are the largest and finest I ever saw. You'll be pleased when I tell you the quarters of the above mentioned little wilderness are filled with these and with cherry trees of the best kinds all within reach of the hand.

At the end of these terraces run two long walks

under the side walls of the garden which communicate with the other terraces that front them opposite. Between, the valley is laid level and divided into two regular groves of horse-chestnuts, and a bowling green in the middle of about 180 foot. This is bounded by a canal, that runs quite across the groves and also along one side, in the form of a T. Behind this, is a semicircular *berceau*, and a thicket of mixed trees that completes the crown of the amphitheatre which is of equal extent with the bowling green.

ALEXANDER POPE

THE HERMIT'S SEAT

On the opposite hanging of the bank (which is a steep of 50 feet) is placed, with a very fine fancy, a rustic seat of stone, flagged and rough, with two urns in the same rude taste upon pedestals, on each side: from whence you lose your eyes upon the glimmering of the waters under the wood, and your ears in the constant dashing of the waves. In view of this, is a bridge that crosses the stream, built in the same ruinous state: the wall of the garden hanging over it, is humoured so as to appear the ruin of another arch or two above the bridge. Hence you mount the hill over the Hermit's Seat (as they call it) described before, and so to the highest terrace again.

ALEXANDER POPE

THE WHITE SEAT

Turn, therefore, at the top of the bank, turn to the left and follow the edge of the slope till it brings you to this angle of the lawn; it is an excellent spot for the beginning of a morning's exploration. Many possibilities here converged; and here, to begin with, stood a wonderful white seat, semi-circular, triply divided, high in the middle and quite low at the sides—an ancient, a historic seat, on which I might well subside for a minute or so, while I try to explain the complication of interest that gathered in this corner. It is not easy at all; so much seems to happen at once, what with the geranium-blaze that here comes shelving up from the lower level, and the red wall, with its cascade of wistaria and clematis, that branches away from a corner of the house and curves like an arm in this direction, and the cool shrubbery rustling behind me, and the glimpse, if I look round, of a sun-bright enclosure, formally laid out, the approach to which is just here, close at hand. It is difficult indeed to make my way methodically; I should remain on the white seat till nightfall, shifting from one to another of its three divisions and back again, if I had to describe how all these diversities fitted together, conjoining at this point.

But there is no hurry, after all; and as I sit there, under the tasselled branch of a larch that leans out from the edge of the shrubbery, I take in afresh the delighted sense of easy abundance, the loose comfort, the soft-bosomed maturity of the garden.

PERCY LUBBOCK

A BROAD TERRACE

My garden should lie to the south of the house; the ground generally sloping for some short way till it falls abruptly into the dark and tangled shrubberies that all but hide the winding brook below. A broad terrace, half as wide, at least, as the house is high, should run along the whole southern length of the building, extending to the western side also, whence, over the distant country, I may catch the last red light of the setting sun. I must have some musk and noisette roses, and jasmine, to run up the mullions of my oriel window, and honeysuckles and clematis, the white, the purple and the blue, to cluster round the top. The upper terrace should be strictly architectural, and no plants are to be harboured there, save such as twine among the balustrades, or fix themselves in the mouldering crevices of the stone. I can endure no plants in pots – a plant in a pot is like a bird in a cage. The gourd alone throws out its vigorous tendrils, and displays its green and golden fruit from the vases that surmount the broad flight of stone steps that lead to the lower terrace; while a vase of larger dimensions and bolder sculpture at the western corner is backed by the heads of a mass of crimson, rose, and straw-coloured hollyhocks that spring up from the bank below. The lower terrace is twice the width of the one above, of the most velvety turf laid out in an elaborate pattern of the Italian style. Here are collected the choicest flowers of the garden, the Dalmatic purple of the gentianella, the dazzling scarlet of the verbena, the fulgent lobelia, the bright yellows and rich browns of the calceolaria here luxuriate in their trimly cut parterres, and with colours as brilliant as the mosaic of an old cathedral's painted window.

But you must leave this mass of gorgeous colouring and the two pretty fountains that play in their basins of native rock, while you descend the flight of steps, simpler than those of the upper terrace, and turn to the left hand, where a broad gravel walk will lead you to the kitchen-garden, through an avenue splendid in autumn with hollyhocks, dahlias, China asters, nasturtians, and African marigolds.

We will stop short of the walled garden to turn among the clipt hedges of box, and yew, and hornbeam which surround the bowling-green, and lead to a curiously formed labyrinth, in the centre of which, perched up on a triangular mound, is a fanciful old summer-house, with a gilded roof, that commands the view of the whole surrounding country.

ANON

SEATS

One of the most talented garden designers of our epoch, the Countess of Rosse, frequently used garden seats as features for the lovely landscapes which she created at Nymans in Sussex, Wormesley House in Yorkshire, or Birr Castle in Ireland. They provide features to terminate vistas because, she claimed, 'There must always be something to beckon the eye, be it a seat, a spectacular plant or some other artefact – sculpture, a fountain or a building.' Her talents as a designer are not confined to landscaping; at Birr she designed a charming wooden garden seat whose decorative back embodies the letters A and M, which are the initials of the Countess and her late husband.

Stationed at the end of an allee in the formal garden, its decorative form perfectly complements the hornbeams whose branches she has trained to resemble rococo vaults. Lady Rosse pointed out that if they beckon the eye from afar, seats logically must present a long view to those sitting on them. 'And people so frequently forget the obvious rule that a seat should never be set anywhere that does not offer an interesting view.'

Few of us have estate carpenters or can commission

personalized bespoke seats. Accurate reproductions of Georgian and Victorian seats are, however, to be found at reasonable prices. So are handsome benches in simulated stone.

But some of my favourite seats have been very simple to make and are not costly. Well sanded, honest chunks of wood, such as railway sleepers, set on brick or stone supports, look well in any surroundings, however sophisticated. Far-sighted garden designers also often find an effective way of building a seat into a wall while it is being constructed. Such arrangements are infinitely preferable to the plastic variety of seat which does not 'weather' and to my mind always looks unwelcome in any garden setting.

White is an appropriate colour for many designs in wood or metal and undoubtedly amplifies their ability to beckon the eye, but I believe that it must be used with great care in a green landscape. It can be intrusive and it can deaden the subtler colours around it. In my experience that traditional dull, dark-green (sometimes called London Green or British Racing Green) is a satisfactory unobtrusive finish for most garden furniture if the natural finish needs protection. I agree with Richard Bolem, the most experienced mason of the famous landscaping contractors, Waterers, when he says, 'After all, it is the plants which should provide most of the colour in a garden.'

Finally, do not forget the nose as well as the eye when placing a seat – place fragrants like lavender, or stock, nearby so that their scents can be enjoyed on still, warm summer evenings, even if, as there were in Henry VIII's time, there are now no 'pestilent ayers' to repulse.

G.R.

Flowerbeds and Borders

COARSE THINGS

Plaintive letters reach me from time to time saying that if I do not like herbaceous borders, what would I put in their place? It is quite true that I have no great love for herbaceous borders or for the plants that usually fill them – coarse things with no delicacy or quality about them. I think the only justification for such borders is that they shall be perfectly planned, both in regard to colour and to grouping; perfectly staked – and perfectly weeded.

VITA SACKVILLE-WEST

WHAT A MESS

It was a blustering day and the wind had taken and broken the dahlias. Mrs Honeychurch, who looked cross, was tying them up, while Miss Bartlett, unsuitably dressed, impeded her with offers of assistance ... 'Gracious what a mess everything is! Look at my scarlet pompoms,' said Mrs Honeychurch. 'And the ground so hard that not a prop will stick in it ... I'm certain that the orange cactus will go before I can get to it.'

E.M. FORSTER

THE BEAUTY OF A FLOWER MEADOW

There sprang the violete al newe,
And fresshe pervinke riche of hewe,
And floures yelowe, whyte and rede:
Swich plentee grew ther never in mede,

Ful gay was al the ground and queynt
And poudred, as men had it peynt,
With many a fresh and sondry flour
That casten up a ful good savour.

GEOFFREY CHAUCER

THE HERBACEOUS BORDER

Merely having plants or having them planted unassorted in garden spaces, is only like having a box of paints from the best colour man; or, to go one step farther, it is like having portions of these paints set out upon a palette. This does not constitute a picture; and it seems to me that the duty we owe to our gardens and to our own bettering of our gardens is so to use the plants that they shall form beautiful pictures; and that, while delighting our eyes, they should be always training those eyes to a more exalted criticism; to a state of mind and artistic conscience that will not tolerate bad or careless combination or any sort of mis-use of plants, but in which it becomes a point of honour to be always striving for the best.

It is just in the way it is done that lies the whole difference between commonplace gardening and gardening that may rightly claim to rank as a fine art.

GERTRUDE JEKYLL

VARIATIONS OF FLOWERS

Variations of flowers are like variations in music, often beautiful as such, but almost always inferior to the theme on which they are founded – the original air. And the rule holds good in beds of flowers, if they be not very large, or in any other small assemblage of them. Nay, the largest bed will look well, if of one beautiful colour; while the most beautiful varieties may be inharmoniously mixed up. Contrast is a good thing, but we should first get a good sense of the thing to be contrasted, and we shall find this preferable to the contrast, if we are not rich enough to have both in good measure. We do not in general love and honour any one single colour enough, and we are instinctively struck with a conviction to this effect when we see it abundantly set forth. The other day we saw a little garden-wall completely covered with nasturtiums, and felt how much more beautiful it was than if anything had been mixed with it. For the leaves, and the light and shade, offer variety enough. The rest is all richness and simplicity united—which is the triumph of an intense perception.

LEIGH HUNT

MIXED BORDERS

There is nothing much more difficult to do in outdoor gardening than to plant a mixed border well, and to keep it in beauty throughout the summer. Every year, as I gain experience, and, I hope, more power of critical judgment, I find myself tending towards broader and simpler effects, both of grouping and colour. I do not know whether it is·by individual preference, or in obedience to some colour-law that I can instinctively feel but cannot pretend even to understand, and much less to explain, but in practice I always find more satisfaction and facility in treating the warm colours (reds and yellows) in graduated harmonies, culminating into gorgeousness, and the cool ones in contrasts; especially in the case of blue, which I like to use either in distinct but not garish contrasts, as of full blue with pale yellow, or in separate cloudlike harmonies, as of lilac and pale purple with grey foliage. I am never so much inclined to treat the blues, purples and lilacs in associated gradations as the reds and yellows. Purples and lilacs I can put together, but not these with blues; and the pure blues always seem to demand peculiar and very careful treatment.

GERTRUDE JEKYLL

FLOWERS

I am left standing by the flowers. It is very early, before lessons. Flower after flower is specked on the depths of green. The petals are harlequins. Stalks rise from the black hollows beneath. The flowers swim like fish made of light upon the dark, green waters. I hold a stalk in my hand. I am the stalk. My roots go down to the depths of the world, through earth dry with brick and damp earth, through veins of lead and silver. I am all fibre. All tremors shake me, and the weight of the earth is pressed to my rib. Up here my eyes are green leaves, unseeing . . .

VIRGINIA WOOLF

PROFUSELY INCONSISTENT

Not a flower could look constrained, unnaturally smartened, in the garden at Earlham; even if they sat up in rows and stripes, they did so with enjoyment unconcerned. They glowed, they revelled; and moreover it was not, in any vulgar sense, a well-kept garden. It was profusely inconsistent; if one flower-bed was stuck over with geraniums like a pin-cushion and rimmed with horrible little monsters of fretted, empurpled foliage, the next might be a bower, a boscage, a ramp of sweet peas, a bushy luxuriance of phlox and rosemary. And especially the border against the slow curve of the wall which I mentioned just now—this was a mazy confusion of everything that gleams and glows and exhales a spicery of humming fragrance. Peacock butterflies, brilliant red admirals, fluttered over the blue mist of sea-lavender; a tree of verbena, the lemon-scented herb of which you pull a leaf whenever you pass, branched out close to the immense old trunk of the wistaria; salvia blue and red, bitter-sweet phloxes white and crimson-eyed, the russet and purple trumpets of the lovely creature afflicted with the name of salpiglossis, they all rejoiced together, rambling and crowding in liberal exuberance. The gardener might wreak his worst will, scheming for a smart patchwork; but the free soul of the garden escaped him and bloomed tumultuously.

PERCY LUBBOCK

BEDS AND BORDERS

Whatever Vita Sackville-West says about them, some of her borders at Sissinghurst are quite stunning, but she was writing after 1945 when time and labour were not available to most of her readers. The herbaceous border had been developed in an earlier, more leisurely and, we must say it, a less democratic, era.

Who actually invented the herbaceous border? I have tried

hard to find a definitive answer to this question.

In the last half of the nineteenth century, garden designers and writers like William Robinson and Gertrude Jekyll were great protagonists, but there is no suggestion that either of them used it first. Some years before their ascendancy, at Arley Hall in Cheshire, one of the earliest herbaceous borders of which I am aware was already in full flare. It is recorded as having flourished in 1845. However its scale was and remains so magnificent that it is unlikely that perennial plants had never previously been assembled in that way, so I believe there must have been smaller-scale and simpler prototype borders.

When at their best, carefully tended and well-ordered, the overall feeling of the summer-flowering border is one of joyous splendour. The gardeners I know who use the rules of border planting with subtlety, are those who triumph. They recall Jekyll's dictum that 'colour in gardening as in painting does not mean a garish or startling effect . . . it means the management of colour with the deliberate intention of producing beautiful pictorial effects whether by means of harmony or of contrast'. In their gardens we are unaware of deliberate planning or ground work – the total effect is that nature has allowed the plants simply to tumble into congenial places where they are happy to express their satisfaction by blooming exuberantly. Their abundance of flowers and their fullness of foliage, subtly mimics that of individual plant clumps stationed among the soft fruit bushes in the typical cottage garden. And it was there, perhaps, that some garden-conscious squire or vicar obtained his inspiration for the creation of the first herbaceous border.

Whatever its origin, it would have to have been invented – if it hadn't existed – by the second half of the nineteenth century, in order to display the wealth of herbaceous plants which began to pour into Europe as a result of plant-hunting expeditions.

Sadly, the sheer volume of manual labour which such a border demanded gradually but inevitably led to its decline. If the 'big houses' could not always afford the labour to dig out and divide plants every other year, to weed scrupulously, and tie and stake assiduously, then the smaller gardener would be bound to ask himself if he had time to manage a border properly. Yet he'd also have to admit that a garden without a herbaceous bed of some sort is a deprived place, with nowhere fully to celebrate the procession of the seasons, from the new shoots of spring to the fading foliage of autumn.

I believe that half the work is caused because gardeners choose plants which are too big and grow too quickly. This is the fault of the plant breeders who for far too long took the view that biggest and brightest was best. The simpler plants used in the earlier herbaceous borders were frequently taken from the wild or still possessed the hardy self-reliant strength of wild ancestors. The answer for us today, I feel, is to select plants from those nurseries which have specialized in the smaller plants which do not have these defects and I have even seen splendid borders with all the recognized herbaceous qualities composed entirely of culinary and medicinal herbs which tend to be fine survivors with very little attention from the gardener.

Ground forest bark will make an attractive mulch over the soil between the clumps of plants, and reduce weeding dramatically. It is also useful in conserving soil moisture and ultimately in increasing its organic content. An original 'mulch' is used in one of my favourite flower gardens, Herterton House, near Cambo in Northumberland, where they make use of a beautiful stone grit taken from the Coquet river nearby. As well as suppressing the weeds, it is a wonderful background for plants of all colours. Other types of grit, gravel and fragments of rock make a perfect background for a scree garden of alpine plants which, as miniature versions of many of our common border plants, will give you the same exciting seasonal evolution as they do.

G.R.

Topiary, Trees and Shrubs

A SATIRE ON TOPIARY

Adam and Eve in Yew; Adam a little shattered by the fall of the tree of knowledge in the great storm; Eve and the serpent very flourishing.

St. George in box; his arm scarce long enough, but will be in condition to stick the dragon by next April.

A green dragon of the same, with a tail of ground ivy for the present.

A laurustine bear in blossom, with a juniper hunter in berries.

A pair of giants, stunted, to be sold cheap.

A Queen Elizabeth in phylyraea a little inclining to the green-sickness, but of full growth.

Another Queen Elizabeth in myrtle, which was very forward, but miscarried by being too near a savine.

An old maid of honour in wormwood. A topping Ben Jonson in Laurel.

Divers eminent modern poets in bays, somewhat blighted, to be disposed of, a pennyworth.

A quick-set hog, shot up into a porcupine, by being forgot a week in rainy weather.

A lavender pig with sage growing in his belly.

Noah's ark in holly, standing on the mount; the ribes a little damaged for want of water.

A pair of maidenheads in fir, in great forwardness.

ALEXANDER POPE

IMAGES BE FOR CHILDREN

For the ordering of the ground within the great hedge, I leave it to variety of device; advising, nevertheless, that whatsoever form you cast it into, first, it be not too busy or full of work. Wherein I, for my part, do not like images cut out in juniper or other garden stuff: they be for children. Little low hedges, round, like welts, with some pretty pyramides, I like well; and in some places, fair columns upon frames of carpenter's work. I would also have the alleys spacious and fair. You may have closer alleys upon the side grounds, but none in the main garden. I wish also, in the very middle, a fair mount, with three ascents, and alleys, enough for four to walk abreast; which I would have to be perfect circles, without any bulwarks or embossments; and the whole mount to be thirty foot high; and some fine banqueting-house, with some chimneys neatly cast, and without too much glass.

FRANCIS BACON

THE ROMANTIC

Vita refuses to abide by our decision or to remove the miserable little trees which stand in the way of my design. The romantic temperament as usual obstructing the classic.

HAROLD NICOLSON

BOX

Many paths are divided from one another by box. In one place you have a little meadow; in another the box is interposed in groups, and cut into a thousand different forms; sometimes into letters expressing the name of the master, or again, that of the artificer; whilst here and there little obelisks rise inter-mixed alternately with

apple trees, when on a sudden, in the midst of this
elegant regularity, you are surprised with an imitation of
the negligent beauties of rural nature; in the centre of
which lies a spot surrounded with a knot of dwarf plane
trees. Beyond these are interspersed clumps of the
smooth and twisting acanthus; then come a variety of
figures and names cut in box.

PLINY

REPLANTING

I carried off from the countries I had conquered trees
that none of my kings, my forefathers had possessed,
these trees I have taken and planted them in mine own
country, in the parks of Assyria have I planted them.

TIGLATH-PILESER

TRANSPORTING

Whenever the Khan receives information of a handsome tree growing in any place he causes it to be dug
up, with all its roots and the earth about them, and
however large and heavy it may be, he has it transported
by means of elephants to this mount and adds it to the
verdant collection. From this perpetual verdure it has
acquired the appellation of the Green Mount ... The
view of this altogether – the mount itself, the trees, and
the buildings form a delightful and at the same time a
wonderful scene ... Equally within the precincts of the
city, there is a large and deep excavation ... the earth
from which supplied the material for raising the mount.
It is furnished with water by a small rivulet and has the

appearance of a fish-pond but is used for watering the cattle.

MARCO POLO

INTERSPERSING

Trees without any order or regularity (but pretty thick as they can at any time be thin'd) and to consist that at the North end, of locusts altogether, and that at the South, of all the clever kind of Trees (especially flowering ones) that can be got, such as Crab apple, Poplar, Dogwood, Sassafras, Laurel, Willow (especially yellow and Weeping Willow) . . . these to be interspersed here and there with ever greens such as Holly, Pine, and Cedar, also Ivy; to these may be added the Wild flowering Shrubs of the larger kind, such as the fringe Tree and several other kinds that might be mentioned.

GEORGE WASHINGTON

SONGS MY FATHER TAUGHT ME

If he could not write about gardens with success, at least he could make them in the world of actuality. He abolished small hills, created lakes, and particularly liked now to alter the levels at which full-grown trees were standing. Two old yew trees in front of the dining-room windows at Renishaw were regularly heightened and lowered; a process which I then believed could have been shown to chart, like a thermometer, the temperature of his mood, and to which he always referred as 'pulling and dragging'. ('That oak tree needs to be pulled and dragged!') From the wooden towers constructed for the purpose in the lake and on the hill he would measure and survey. His head throbbed with ideas, the majority of them never to be put into practice. Glass fountains, aqueducts in rubble, gigantic figures, cascades through the woods, stone boats and dragons in the water of lake and pool, blue-stencilled white cows 'to give distinction to the landscape', many of these schemes, alas, remained where they were born. But they were a fine exercise for him, and a diversion.

OSBERT SITWELL

WHEN LILACS LAST IN THE DOORYARD BLOOM'D

In the dooryard fronting an old farm-house near the
    white-wash'd palings,
Stands the lilac-bush tall-growing with heart-shaped
    leaves of rich green,
With many a pointed blossom rising delicate, with the
    perfume strong I love,
With every leaf a miracle—and from this bush in the
    dooryard,
With delicate-color'd blossoms and heart-shaped leaves
    of rich green,
A sprig with its flower I break.

WALT WHITMAN

SHADE IS OUR ELYSIUM

The grounds . . . I destine to improve in the style of the English gardens . . . Their sunless climate has permit-

49

ted them to adopt what is certainly a beauty of the very first order in landscape. Their canvas is of open ground, variegated with clumps of trees distributed with taste. They need no more of wood than will serve to embrace a lawn or a glade. But under the beaming, constant, and almost vertical sun of Virginia, shade is our Elysium. In the absence of this no beauty of the eye can be enjoyed ... The only substitute I have been able to imagine is this: Let your ground be covered with trees of the loftiest stature. Trim up their bodies so high as the constitution and form of the tree will bear, but so as that their tops shall unite and yield dense shade. A wood so open below, will have nearly the appearancee of open grounds.

THOMAS JEFFERSON

HOLLYHOCKS AS BIG AS TREES

Roses red, star-drunken reel
   Over trim white garden paths,
   White roses in the trellis laths
Glowing bosoms half reveal;

Naiad-blue, frail, dancing bells
   Ring a jingle-jingle rhyme
   Faint upon the edge of thyme,
And the proud, plump lily swells.

Iris like a goddess bold
   Purple drapes her beauty so
   That her magic men may know
From her still pool rising cold;

Scarlet Salvias swoon and drift
    Heavy with their maddening bloom,
    Silver sanctuaries of gloom
Their heads the dew-sheathed peonies lift.

These drunken Pagans sing all night,
    All but an enchanted row
    Of hollyhocks that grow and grow
By the house-wall out of sight.

Not a sound or note they make,
    But they're growing, growing fast,
    Skywards they are marching, past
Pinks and floxgloves in their wake.

Pilgrim soldiers you I fear
    In the midnight deep and still
    As you mount the dark blue hill
Of the steep sky shining clear;

Your marching is an aweful hymn
    In the garden of delight,
    In the mad, delirious night,
Giant and lonely Cherubim!

When the Sun comes you shall show
    Great white wings and nimbus gold,
    And your glory we'll behold
From the garden far below.

W.J. TURNER

TREES TO DEFEND BATHERS

And all the margent round about was set
   With shady Laurell trees, thence to defend
   The sunny beames, which on the bellows bet,
   And those which therein bathed, mote offend.
   As Guyon hapned by the same to wend,
   Two naked Damzelles he therein espyde,
   Which therein bathing, seemed to contend
   And wrestle wantonly, ne car'd to hyde
Their dainty parts from vew of any, which them eyde.

Sometimes the one would lift the other quight
   Above the waters, and then doune againe
   Her plong, as over maistered by might,
   Where loth awhile would covered remaine,
   And each the other from to rise restraine;
   The whiles their snowly limbes, as through a vele
   So through the Christall waves appeared plaine:
   Then suddeinly both would themselves unueile
And th' amorous sweet spoiles to greedy eyes reuele.

As that faire Starre, the messenger of morne,
   His deawy face out of the sea doth reare:
   Or as the Cyprian goddesse newly borne
   Of th' Ocean's fruitfull froth, did first appeare:
   Such seemed they, and so their yellow heare
   Christalline humour droppeth doune apace.
   Upon such when Guyon saw, he drew him neare,
   And somewhat gan relent his earnest pace,
His stubborne brest gan secret pleasaunce to embrace.

EDMUND SPENSER

TOPIARY

Alexander Pope was no mean satirist, and when he turned his mocking eye on the neglected or incomplete topiary around him, the result is key reading for modern gardeners who have attempted the art. My favourite is this:

> *A quick-set hog*, shot up into a porcupine, by being forgot a week in rainy weather.

I would love to hear what he would have said if faced with my own past attempts to create hawthorn crowing cockerels which turned out to be wrens with broken wings. Since those failures, I have turned my attention, more successfully, to what I like to think of as 'soft masonry'. This is shorthand for applying simple topiary techniques using the secateur and the electric clipper to thick hedges of yew, privet, hawthorn or conifers like the lawson cypress or *Cupressocyparis leylandi* so as to cut and maintain simple architectural forms. Gateways with arches above and protruding pilasters to support them do not present great difficulties for the amateur. Unlike the animals and birds, they do not require all those complex curves or rounded forms. And I suggest that gardeners should try them because a hedge treated in this way provides a very satisfactory halfway barrier between the rigidity of a brick or stone wall and the informality of a loose hedge. Instead of just providing a low-browed tunnel through the hedge, one can enoble it to become a feature as well as an entrance to another area of the garden.

Some of the most inspiring examples of this approach I have seen were in the garden of the Villa Noailles near Grasse in the south of France. These included not only green gateways, but also massive windbreaks for garden seats every bit as impressive as a stage set at Covent Garden.

G.R.

Greenhouses,
Summerhouses
and Conservatories

MAGIC*

I love a still conservatory
   That's full of giant, breathless palms,
Azaleas, clematis and vines,
   Whose quietness great Trees becalms
Filling the air with foliage,
   A curved and dreamy statuary.

I like to hear a cold, pure rill
   Of water trickling low, afar
With sudden little jerks and purls
   Into a tank or stoneware jar,
The song of a tiny sleeping bird
   Held like a shadow in its trill.

I love the mossy quietness
   That grows upon the great stone flags,
The dark tree-ferns, the staghorn ferns,
   The prehistoric, antlered stags
That carven stand and stare among
   The silent, ferny wilderness.

And are they birds or souls that flit
   Among the trees so silently,
And are they fish or ghosts that haunt
   The still pools of the rockery!—
For I am but a sculptured rock
   As in that magic place I sit.

Still as a great jewel is the air
   With boughs and leaves smooth-carved in it,
And rocks and trees and giant ferns,
   And blooms with inner radiance lit,

And naked water like a nymph
   That dances tireless slim and bare.

W.J. TURNER

*There are at least two versions of this poem

A SUFFICIENT QUANTITY OF AIR

To the Rev. John Newton, September 18, 1784
My dear friend,

Following your good example, I lay before me a sheet of my largest paper. It was this moment fair and unblemished but I have begun to blot it, and having begun, am not likely to cease till I have spoiled it. I have sent you many a sheet that in my judgment of it has been very unworthy of your acceptance, but my conscience was in some measure satisfied by reflecting, that if it were good for nothing, at the same time it cost you nothing, except the trouble of reading it. But the case is altered now. You must pay a solid price for frothy matter, and though I do not absolutely pick your pocket, yet you lose your money, and, as the saying is, are never the wiser; a saying literally fulfilled to the reader of my epistles.

My greenhouse is never so pleasant as when we are just upon the point of being turned out of it. The gentleness of the autumnal suns, and the calmness of this latter season, make it a much more agreeable retreat that we ever find it in summer; when, the winds being generally brisk, we cannot cool it by admitting a sufficient quantity of air, without being at the same time incommoded by it. But now I sit with all the windows and door wide open, and am regaled with the scent of every flower in a garden as full of flowers as I have known how to make it. We keep no bees, but if I lived in a hive I should hardly hear more of their music. All the bees in the neighbourhood resort to a bed of mignonette, opposite to the window, and pay me for the honey they get out of it by a hum, which, though rather monotonous, is as agreeable to my ear as the whistling of my linnets. All the sounds that nature utters are delightful—at least in this country.

WILLIAM COWPER

MY SUMMER-ROOM

It was a glorious June morning; and I got up gay and bright, as the Americans say, to breakfast in the pretty summer-room overlooking the garden, which, built partly for my accommodation and partly for that of my geraniums, is as regularly called the green-house as if I and my several properties—sofas, chairs, tables, chiffonières, and ottomans—did not inhabit it during the whole of the fine season; as if it were not in its own person a well-proportioned and spacious apartment, no otherways to be distinguished from common drawing-rooms than by being nearly fronted with glass, about which out-of-door myrtles, passion-flowers, clematis, and the Persian honeysuckle, form a most graceful and varied frame-work, not unlike the festoons of flowers and foliage which one sees round some of the scarce and high-priced tradesmen's cards, and ridotto tickets of Hogarth and Bartolozzi. Large glass folding-doors open into the little garden, almost surrounded by old buildings of the most picturesque form—the buildings themselves partly hidden by clustering vines, and my superb bay-tree, its shining leaves glittering in the sun

57

on one side, whilst a tall pear-tree, garlanded to the very top with an English honeysuckle in full flower, breaks the horizontal line of the low cottage-roof on the other; the very pear-tree being, in its own turn, half concealed by a splendid pyramid of geraniums erected under its shade. Such geraniums! It does not become us poor mortals to be vain—but really, my geraniums! There is certainly nothing but the garden into which Aladdin found his way, and where the fruit was composed of gems, that can compare with them. This pyramid is undoubtedly the great object from the green-house; but the common flower-beds which surround it, filled with roses of all sorts, and lilies of all colours, and pinks of all patterns, and campanulas of all shapes, to say nothing of the innumerable tribes of annuals, of all the outlandish names that were ever invented, are not to be despised even beside the gorgeous exotics, which, arranged with the nicest attention to colour and form, so as to combine the mingled charms of harmony and contrast, seem to look down proudly on their humble compeers.

MARY RUSSELL MITFORD

SEVERAL PAVILIONS

I have built a garden where at my leisure I may find repose and hold converse with my friends. Twenty acres is all the space I need. In the middle is a large summer house, where I have brought together my five thousand books, so as to consult the wisdom therein and to commune with antiquity. On the south side there is a pavilion in the middle of the water, by whose side runs a stream which flows down from the hills. On the east the waters make a deep pond, whence they part in five branches like a leopard's claws. Numbers of swans swim there and are always playing about. At the border of the first stream which falls in cascades, there stands a steep rock with overhanging top like an elephant's trunk. At the summit stands a pleasant open pavilion where people may rest, and where they can enjoy, any morning, the red sunrise . . .

Several pavilions are on the north of the large summer house, scattered about here and there; some of them are on hills, one above the other, standing like a mother amongst her children, while others are on the slopes. Several of them are in little gaps made by the hills, and only half of them can be seen at one time.

HSI MA-KUANG

CONSERVATORIES

Turner's poem first appeared in *Georgian Poetry* in the reign of George V, along with the work of such literary figures as Rupert Brooke, W.H. Davies, John Drinkwater and D.H. Lawrence, but somehow it calls to mind a conservatory of Victorian and Edwardian days – the great days of glass – and the substantial house to which it was attached. Turner in fact lived in Australia until he was seventeen, and he then came to England where he set up as a literary gentleman, and became poet, critic, editor and novelist. He died in 1946, so he neither lived in the great age of the conservatory or survived to see its renaissance.

The notion of creating a protected and controlled environment for plants arose when the homes of the powerful became more domesticated in the late sixteenth century and the land about them began to be used as gardens. Wishing to grow the orange trees which they had seen on their travels in Spain, they built light halls – orangeries – into which the boxes in which they grew could be carried in winter. Sheer greed and an under-standable desire to vary their diet led to the next refinement – the introduction of heat and the evolution of the stove house – and ingenious methods were devised such as channelling chimneys along intricate tunnels inside the walls. This enabled exotica like pineapples and tomatoes – discovered in the New World and the Indies – to be grown and ripened in Northern Britain; and traditional fruits, wild strawberries, pears and apricots, could be ripened early.

These early stoves were usually located in the walled kitchen garden, well away from the house, and had a distinctly utilitarian aspect. Then in the nineteenth century, the plant hunters were sent out to explore the remoter areas of the world to bring back plants, many of which would have to be grown indoors, and this vastly increased the range of ornamental herbaceous plants, shrubs and trees. And so it was that the Victorians realized that more delightful ornamental plants could be enjoyed at home if they built heated glasshouses to take them.

These houses had to be beautiful in themselves to show off plants grown purely for the pleasure of their appearance – and they had to be attached to the ground floor of the main house so that the enjoyment was available all winter long. After the great exhibition of 1851, when the engineer Paxton had demonstrated how well newer materials like cast-iron and glass could be used for ambitious structures, conservatory design developed into a high art. Few houses with any pretension to style were without one, and some of the greatest of Victorian architectural achievements were the result.

Then came the 1914–18 war, and the shortage of man- (or maid-) power to tend the pampered plants, so by the 1930s the majority of Victorian conservatories had tumbled into disrepair or were abandoned. The ubiquitous 'sun lounge', that almost mandatory addition to the homes of a bungalow-owning democracy, while no aesthetic substitute for the conservatory, certainly fulfills some of its functions. Happily, its commercial success has stimulated two significant developments. Lean-to glasshouse manufacturers have realized that there is a good market for more attractive versions of their products and have started to produce them with pleasantly curved glazed roofs. Although still rather bleak, a minimum of softening decoration can be applied (anodized aluminium foil can be stuck directly to the glazing panels to make decorative margins which simulate the patterns of carved wood or cast iron). This, together with wickerwork or bamboo furniture and a spectacular arrangement of bold plants in tubs, enable us to arrive at something approaching the atmosphere of the Victorian conservatory.

The other development has been glass-fibre reinforced plastic mouldings which mimic on a smaller scale the splendours of the Victorian age. Costing little more than the conventional 'sun lounge', they are infinitely more pleasing. And for those who can afford it, there is still a small number of companies endowed with craftsmen of skill to build genuine old-style large-scale conservatories in timber. A compromise is sometimes possible by designing a stylish conservatory made up of standard panels which can be bought at mass-produced prices.

No matter which of these solutions is chosen, the problem that must be overcome is how to heat on dull days in the winter and through the cold nights. Radiators from the house central-heating system can be fitted with thermostatic valves to ensure that the temperature never drops much below 40 degrees fahrenheit. Alternatively, unobtrusive and high-efficiency gas heaters with thermostatic valves are available, and can be cheaper to run and more flexible. Only a few gardeners will be able to afford sufficient heat to grow the plants which thrive in the hottest tropics, but a conservatory can be a joy if near-hardy plants like bougainvillaea can be established.

G.R.

Lawns and
Formal Gardens

LAWNS

My men like satyrs grazing on the lawns
Shall with their goat-feet dance the antic hay.

CHRISTOPHER MARLOWE

The shadows stretched farther and farther across the lawns, and as the sun declined the level light picked out among the grasses innumerable stipplings of shadow; and in the paths, that had seemed under the more perpendicular rays as a table, a thousand little shadowy depressions and sun-touched mountains were now apparent.

ALDOUS HUXLEY

The lawn is a living fossil in a modern human zoo.

WILLIAM KENDRICK

GRASS KEPT FINELY SHORN

For gardens (speaking of those which are indeed prince-like, as we have done of buildings), the contents ought not to be well under thirty acres of ground, and to be divided into three parts: a green in the entrance; a heath or desert in the going forth; and the main garden in the midst; besides alleys on both sides. And I like well that four acres of ground be assigned to the green; six to the heath; four and four to either side; and twelve to the main garden. The green hath two pleasures: the one, because nothing is more pleasant to the eye than green grass kept finely shorn; the other, because it will give you a fair alley in the midst, by which you may go in front upon a stately hedge, which is to enclose the garden. But because the alley will be long, and, in great heat of the year or day, you ought not to buy the shade in the garden by going in the sun through the green, therefore you are, of either side the green, to plant a covert alley, upon carpenter's work, about twelve foot in height, by which you may go in shade into the garden. As for the making of knots or figures with divers-coloured earths, that they may lie under the windows of the house on that side which the garden stands, they be but toys: you may see as good sights many times in tarts.

FRANCIS BACON

RHYTHMIC DANCES IN THE DEW

I went to the door and looked out. I could hardly believe that it was really morning. But it was, and a dashed good morning, at that. The air was cool and fresh, there were long shadows across the lawn, and everything combined to give the soul such a kick that many fellows in my position would have taken off their socks and done rythmic dances in the dew. I did not actually do that, but I certainly felt uplifted to no little extent, and you might say that I was simply so much pure spirit, without any material side to me whatsoever, when suddenly it was as if the old tum had come out of a trance with a jerk, and the next moment I was feeling that nothing mattered in this world or the next except about a quart of coffee and all the eggs and b. you could cram on to a dish!

P.G. WODEHOUSE

THE SMOOTHEST LAWNS
IN THE WORLD

When after sitting a while in a charming modern drawing room, one stepped thoughtlessly through an open window upon a verandah, one found that the horizon of the morning call had been wonderfully widened ... there were the smoothest lawns in the world stretching down to the edge of the liquid slowness and making, where the water touched them, a line as even as the rim of a champagne glass ... The place was a garden of delight ... Just across the river was a level meadow, which rivalled the lawn on which I stood, and this meadow seemed only the more essentially a part of the scene by reason of the voluminous sheep that were grazing on it. These sheep were by no means mere edible mutton; they were poetic, historic, romantic sheep; they were not there for their weight or their wool, they were there for their compositional value, and they visibly knew it.

HENRY JAMES

NOISY DAISIES

'Didn't you know *that*?' cried another Daisy, and here they all began shouting together, till the air seemed quite full of little shrill voices. 'Silence, every one of you!' cried the Tiger-lily, waving itself passionately from side to side, and trembling with excitement. 'They know I can't get at them!' it panted, bending its quivering head towards Alice, 'or they wouldn't dare to do it!'

'Never mind!' Alice said in a soothing tone, and

stooping down to the daisies, who were beginning again, she whispered, 'If you don't hold your tongues, I'll pick you!'

There was silence in a moment, and several of the pink daisies turned white.

'That's right!' said the Tiger-lily. 'The daisies are worst of all. When one speaks, they all begin together, and it's enough to make one wither to hear the way they go on!'

CHARLES DODGSON/LEWIS CARROLL

Dark ages clasp the daisy root.

JAMES JOYCE

THE MEMSAHIB'S LAWN

An Indian attempt at the English lawn was assiduously cultivated. 'Our lawns were made of a special kind of creeping grass, which we used to call *doob* grass. It made the most lovely lawn, so close it smothered most of the weeds. Of course, very often the rest of the compound was bare and hard.' Most lawns required constant irrigation and attendance: 'A little party of three or four men would spread out with a yard or two between them and go up and down the lawn on their hunkers, each man picking out a weed, with another man behind him with a basket egging him on. It was a nice way of mowing one's lawn.'

PLAIN TALES FROM THE RAJ

THE GREAT LAWNS

It was superb, the great lawn at Earlham – it really was. I have described how it was lifted up, almost to the level, I should think, of the first-floor windows, by a steep bank of shaven grass; but there was a considerable expanse on the lower level too, before you reached the bank. On this lower lawn, to right and left, there was a fantastic medley of flower-beds, cut in queer shapes, coils and lozenges and loops; and the gardener's fancy ran strangely riot, year by year, in selecting and disposing the flowers that filled them. Geraniums roasting-red, French marigolds orange and mahogany-coloured, the tomato-note of waxen begonias, exotic herbage all speckled and pied and ring-straked, dahlias, calceolarias – they were marshalled and massed together, they fought it out as they would. But indeed they were mastered by the sunshine, by the blaze of light in which they flashed and twinkled; and they fell back, right and left, leaving a wide space of clear clean grass unbroken. And then there rose before you the green bank, so steep that I wonder how the mowing-machine contrived to sidle along it and keep it thus smoothly shaven.

PERCY LUBBOCK

LAWNS FOR CROQUET

The glory of the Small House at Allington certainly consists in its lawn, which is as smooth, as level, and as much like velvet as grass has ever yet been made to look. Lily Dale, taking pride in her own lawn, has declared often that it is no good attempting to play croquet up at the Great House. The grass, she says, grows in tufts, and nothing that Hopkins, the gardener, can or will do has any effect upon the tufts. But there are no tufts at the Small House. As the squire himself has never been very enthusiastic about croquet, the croquet implements have been moved permanently down to the Small House, and croquet there has become quite an institution.

ANTHONY TROLLOPE

THE MAKING OF KNOTS FOR A GARDEN

... either with Germander, Issope, Time, or Pinke-Gilly-flowres , but of all hearbes Germander is the most principallest best for this purpose: divers do use in Knots to set Thrift, and in time of need it may serve, but it is not so good as any of the other, because it is much more subject to be slaine with frost, and will also spread upon the earth in such sort that, without very painefull cutting, it will put your Knot out of fashion.

GERVASE MARKHAM

LAWNS – FORMAL GARDENS

Despite the reverence which they inspire or the attention which they receive, extensive, unrelieved, formally shaped lawns can be very tedious without a suitable setting. They are at their best when surrounded by, or studded with, noble trees which act as splendid horizontal screens for the shadow play of foliage on sunny days.

One good way of relieving the boredom which a large lawn can provoke, if the general topography of the land permits, is to arrange it on two levels so as to create a sunken rectangle or a shallow grass amphitheatre. The levels can be connected by gentle grass slopes which, to increase interest and avoid problems of frequent mowing, can be sown as a flower meadow. Using the right mixture of attractive meadow grasses and wildflower seed supplemented by a generous planting of bulbs, the area connecting the two levels of mown lawn can be a carpet of exciting shapes and attractive colour throughout the season.

But even without this type of rustic relief, formal lawns can be greatly improved by stressing their formality. Surrounding them completely with well laid, high-quality paving can provide a very satisfying lawn frame. These formally paved paths or surrounds usually need some vertical features if they are not to look too harsh. Happily nowadays, apart from terra-cotta urns and vases, there are small-scaled simulated stone items available such as cubes, spheres, pyramids, cones and obelisques, which allow people with small gardens to endow them with a formality which would seem ludicrous if they had to rely upon reproductions of large eighteenth-century garden ornaments. The latter were intended to garnish the landscapes surrounding mansions, not the more modest gardens of the present day.

G.R.

Paradise and Arcady

OF GARDENS

God Almighty first planted a garden. And indeed it is the purest of human pleasures. It is the greatest refreshment to the spirits of man; without which, buildings and palaces are but gross handyworks: and a man shall ever see that when ages grow to civility and elegancy, men come to build stately sooner than to garden finely; as if gardening were the greater perfection. I do hold it, in the royal ordering of gardens, there ought to be gardens for all the months in the year; in which, severally, things of beauty may then be in season. For December and January and the latter part of November, you must take such things as are green all winter: holly; ivy; bays; juniper; cypress-trees; yew; pine-apple-trees; fir-trees; rosemary; lavender; periwinkle, the white, the purple, and the blue; germander; flags; orange-trees, lemon-trees, and myrtles, if they be stoved; and sweet marjoram, warm set. There followeth, for the latter part of January and February, the mezereon-tree, which then blossoms; crocus vernus, both the yellow and the gray; primroses; anemones; the early tulipa; hyacinthus orientalis; chamaïris; fritillaria. For March, there come violets, specially the single blue, which are the earliest; the yellow daffodil; the daisy; the almond-tree in blossom; the peach-tree in blossom; the cornelian-tree in blossom; sweet briar. In April follow, the double white violet; the wall-flower; the stock-gillyflower; the cowslip; flower-delices, and lilies of all natures; rosemary flowers; the tulippa; the double piony; the pale daffodil; the French honeysuckle; the cherry-tree in blossom; the dammasin and plum-trees in blossom; the white-thorn in leaf; the lilac-tree. In May and June come pinks of all sorts, especially the blush pink; roses of all kinds, except the musk, which comes later; honeysuckles; strawberries; bugloss; columbine; the French marygold; flos Africanus; cherry-tree in fruit; ribes; figs in fruit; rasps; vine flowers; lavender in flower; the sweet satyrian, with the white flower; herba muscaria; lilium convallium; the apple-tree in blossom. In July come gillyflowers of all varieties; musk-roses; the lime-tree in blossom; early pears and plums in fruit; ginitings; quadlins. In August come plums of all sorts in fruit; pears; apricocks; berberries; filberds; musk-melons; monkshoods, of all colours. In September come grapes; apples; poppies of all colours; peaches; melocotones; nectarines; cornelians; wardens; quinces. In October and the beginning of November come services; medlars, bullises; roses cut or removed to come late; hollyokes; and such like. These particulars are for the climate of London; but my meaning is perceived, that you may have *ver perpetuum*, as the place affords.

FRANCIS BACON

PARADISE LOST

. . . Thus was this place
A happy rural seat of various view:
Groves whose rich trees wept odorous gums and balm,
Others whose fruit burnish'd with golden rind
Hung amiable, Hesperian fables true,
If true, here only, and of delicious taste.
Betwixt them lawns, or level downs, and flocks
Grazing the tender herb, were interposed,
Or palmy hillock, or the flow'ry lap
Of some irriguous valley spread her store,

Flow'rs of all hue, and without thorn the rose.
Another side, umbrageous grots and caves
Of cool recess, o'er which the mantling vine
Lays forth her purple grape, and gently creeps
Luxuriant: meanwhile murmuring waters fall
Down the slope hills, dispersed, or in a lake,
That to the fringèd bank with myrtle crown'd
Her crystal mirror holds, unite their streams.
The birds their choir apply; airs, vernal airs,
Breathing the smell of field and grove, attune
The trembling leaves, while universal Pan,
Knit with the Graces and the Hours in dance,
Led on th' eternal spring. Not that fair field
Of Enna, where Proserpine gathering flow'rs,
Herself a fairer flow'r, by gloomy Dis.

JOHN MILTON

PERSIAN PARADISE

Everywhere the Persian king is zealously cared for, so
that he may find gardens wherever he goes; their name
is *Paradise* and they are full of all things fair and good
that the earth can bring forth.

XENOPHON

WHERE PARADISE WAS

If we believe the Scripture, we must allow that God
Almighty esteemed the life of a man in a garden the
happiest He could give him, or else He would not have
placed Adam in that of Eden; that it was the state of
innocence and pleasure; and that the life of husbandry

and cities came after the Fall, with guilt and with labour.

Where Paradise was, has been much debated, and little agreed.

SIR WILLIAM TEMPLE

THE GARDEN OF CYRUS

Nebuchodonosor whom some will have to be the famous *Syrian* King of *Diodorus* ... so magnificently built his hanging gardens, that from succeeding Writers he had the honour of the first. From whence overlooking *Babylon*, and all the region about it, he found no circumscription to the eye of his ambition, till over-delighted with the bravery of this Paradise; in his melancholy metamorphosis, he found the folly of that delight, and a proper punishment, in the contrary habitation, in wild plantations and wanderings of the fields.

The *Persian* Gallants who destroyed this Monarchy, maintained their Botanicall bravery. Unto whom we owe the very name of Paradise: wherewith we meet not in Scripture before the time of *Solomon*, and conceived originally *Persian*. The word for that disputed Garden, expressing in the Hebrew no more than a Field enclosed.

Cyrus the elder, brought up in Woods and Mountains, when time and power enabled, pursued the dictate of his education, and brought the treasures of the field into rule and circumscription. So nobly beautifying the hanging Gardens of *Babylon*, that he was also thought to be the author thereof.

Abasuerus (whom many conceive to have been *Artaxerxes Longi-manus*) in the Countrey and City of

Flowers, and in an open Garden, entertained his Princes and people . . .

But if (as some opinion) King *Abasuerus* were *Artaxerxes Mnemon*, that found a life and reign answerable unto his great memory, our magnified *Cyrus* was his second Brother . . . A person of high spirit and honour, naturally a King, though fatally prevented by the harmlesse chance of *post*-geniture: Not only a Lord of Gardens, but a manuall planter thereof: disposing his trees, like his armies in regular ordination. So that while old *Laertes* hath found a name in Homer for pruning hedges, and clearing away thorns and bryars, while King *Attalus* lives for his poysonous plantations of *Aconites*, Henbane, Hellabore, and plants hardly admitted within the walls of Paradise: While many of the Ancients do poorly live in the single names of Vegetables: All stories do look upon *Cyrus* as the splendid and regular planter.

SIR THOMAS BROWNE

PARADISE AT STOWE

It puzzles much the sages' brains,
    Where Eden stood of yore;
Some place it in Arabia's plains;
    Some say it is no more.

But Cobham can these tales confute,
    As all the curious know;
For he had prov'd beyond dispute,
    That Pàradise is Stowe.

NATHANIEL COTTON

The first of August we went to Stowe, which is beyond
description; it gives the best idea of Paradise that can
be: even Milton's images and descriptions fall short of
it; and indeed a Paradise it must be to every mind in a
state of tolerable innocence. Without the soul's sunshine every object is dark; but a contented mind, in so
sweet a situation must feel the most 'sober certainty of
waking bliss'. The buildings are indeed, in themselves,
disagreeably crowded, but being dedicated to patriots,
heroes, law-givers, and poets, and men of ingenuity and
invention, they receive a dignity from the persons to
whom they are consecrated. Others, that are sacred to
imaginary powers, raise a pleasing enthusiasm in the
mind.

MRS ELIZABETH MONTAGU

MY LITTLE EDEN

'My little plot,' said Miss Mapp. 'Very modest, as you
see, three-quarters of an acre at the most, but well
screened. My flower-beds: sweet roses, tortoise-shell
butterflies. Rather a nice clematis. My Little Eden I call
it, so small, but so well beloved.'

'Enchanting!' said Lucia, looking round the garden
before mounting the steps up to the garden-room door.
There was a very green and well-kept lawn, set in bright
flower-beds. A trellis at one end separated it from a
kitchen-garden beyond, and round the rest ran high
brick walls, over which peered the roofs of other houses.
In one of these walls was cut a curved archway with a
della Robbia head above it.

'Shall we just pop across the lawn,' said Miss Mapp,
pointing to this, 'and peep in there while Withers brings

our tea? Just to stretch the – the limbs, Mrs Lucas, after your long drive. There's a wee little plot beyond there which is quite a pet of mine. And here's sweet Puss-Cat come to welcome my friends. Lamb! Love-bird!'

Love-bird's welcome was to dab rather crossly at the caressing hand which its mistress extended, and to trot away to ambush itself beneath some fine hollyhocks where it regarded them with singular disfavour.

E.F. BENSON

A FRENCH PARADISE

I this day finish'd with a walke in the greate garden of the Thuilleries, rarely contriv'd for privacy, shade, or company, by groves, plantations of tall trees, especially that in the middle, being of elmes, the other of mulberys; and that labyrinth of cypresse; not omitting the noble hedges of pomegranates, fountaines, fish-ponds, and an aviary; but above all the artificial echo, redoubling the words so distinctly, and as it is never without some faire nymph singing to its grateful returns: standing at one of the focus's, which is under a tree, or little cabinet of hedges, the voice seems to descend from the clouds; at another as if it was underground. This being at the botome of the garden, we were let into another, which was being kept with all imaginable accuratenesse in reguard of the orangery, precious shrubes, and rare fruites, seem'd a paradise.

JOHN EVELYN

A PLACE CALLED PARADISE

Catalonapes . . . had a fair castel on a hil & strong, & he made a wal all about the hil right strong & fayre, within he had a faire gardeine wherin were many trees bearing all maner of fruits that he might fynd, & he had planted therin al maner of herbs of good smel & that bare flowers, & ther wer many faire wels, . . . & he had in his gardeine all thing that might be to man solace & comfort, he had also in that gardeine maydens within the age of XV yeare, the fairest that he might find, & men children of the same age, & they were clothed with clothes of gold, & he sayd that they were aungels and he caused to be made certain hils, & enclosed them about with precious stones of Jaspy & christal & set in gold & pearls, and other maner of stones, and he had made a coundute under the earth, so that whan he wold the wals ran somtime with milke, somtime honey, & this place is called Paradise.

SIR JOHN MANDEVILLE

AN ORCHARD AND GARDEN

What was Paradise? But a Garden and Orchard of trees and herbs, full of all pleasure? And nothing there but delights. The gods of the Earth, resembling the great God of heaven in authoritie, Magestie, and abundance of all things, wherein is their most delight? And whither doe they withdraw themselves from the troublesome affayres of their estate, being tyred with the hearing and judging of litigious Controversies? choked (as it were), with the close ayres of their sumptious buildings, their stomacks cloyed with varietie of Banquets, their eares filled and over-burthened with tedious discoursings.

Whither? but into their Orchards? made and prepared, dressed and destinated for that purpose to renew and refresh their sences, and to call home their over-wearied spirits. Nay, it is (no doubt) a comfort to them, to open their Cazements into a most delicate Garden and Orchard, whereby they may not only see that, wherein they are so much delighted, but also to give fresh, sweete, and pleasant ayre to their Galleries and Chambers.

What can your eye desire to see, your eares to heare, your mouth to taste, or your nose to smell, that is not to be had in an Orchard? with abundance and variety? What more delightsome than an infinite varietie of sweet smelling flowers? decking with sundry colours the greene mantle of the Earth, the universall Mother of us all, so by them bespotted, so dyed, that all the world cannot sample them, and wherein it is more fit to admire the Dyer, than to imitate his workemanship. Colouring not onley the Earth, but decking the ayre and sweetning every breath and spirit.

WILLIAM LAWSON

EARLY GARDEN IN AMERICA

I have just mentioned a garden, and will tell you, that this at Schawfield is the only thing deserving the name I have seen in this country, and laid out with some taste. I could not keep smiling however at the appearance of a soil, that seemed to me no better than dead sand, proposed for a garden. But a few weeks convinced me that I judged very falsely, for the quickness of the vegetation is absolutely astonishing. Nature, to whose care everything is left, does a vast deal; but I remember to have read, tho I forget where, that Adam when he was turned out of paradise, was allowed to carry seeds with him of those fruits he had been suffered to eat of when there, but found on trial that the curse had extended even to them; for they were harsh and very unpalatable, far different from what he had eaten there in his happy state. [Adam is visited by a compassionate Angel who says]: 'The ground has been cursed for your sake and the thorns and briers it must bring forth, and you must eat your bread with the sweat of your brow, yet the curse does not extend to your labours, and it yet depends on your own choice to live in plenty or in penury. Patience and industry will get the better of every difficulty, and the ground will only bear thistles while your indolence permits it . . .' Adam bowed in grateful acknowledgement.

JANET SCHAW

PARADISE, ARCADY, EDEN

The concept of Paradise, Arcady or Eden has persisted throughout history. While its trappings may have changed to suit the style of an epoch, it has nearly always been conceived within the framework of a garden. And it embodies common garden features which are easy to define.

Above all a feeling of total privacy and security must prevail. Nothing truly mundane which could in any way act as a reminder of daily life ever intrudes. The contemplation of weighty philosophic problems; deep consideration of the relationship between man and his world, or man and god; abstract speculation about the baffling conundrums posed by nature, or simply the unabashed enjoyment of erotic notions or sensations, should all be possible without interruption in a true Paradise. It is scarcely possible to imagine such Arcady without balmy air laden with a sweet fragrance of flowers, the murmur of zephyrs through foliage, the lulling buzz of bees or harmonious birdsong. The light, too, must be special. Shafts of sunlight penetrating deep blue shadow must dapple the ground, make dew sparkle and point up a light haze on the distant open ground.

This is easy enough to describe but much harder to achieve, because any feeling that man has intervened substantially could make the Paradise seem merely theatrical. Paradise is often best sought in ancient orchards which have fallen out of production, and where, following their own whims, moss-robed trees have long grown out of their cultured forms. But, sadly, being ripped by the claws of bramble or seared by the venom of the nettles is not an Arcadian experience. Nevertheless gardeners wishing to sponsor the Arcadian feeling could do worse than start in an old orchard. Its surrounding hedge should be thickened by very discreet pruning and planting further quick growers just within the boundary.

Spot applications with selective weedkillers, if repeated for a few seasons, will kill out such treacherous plants as thistles, brambles and nettles. Meanwhile the existing vegetation can be enriched without it seeming as though man the gardener has intervened. Patches of sod can be removed and the soil below can be sown with the seed of the prettiest wildflowers which will spread everywhere if given this good start.

Clumps of perennial herbaceous plants like mombretia, lupins, irises, golden rod or michaelmas daisies can be established in planting holes and will thrive if they are protected from the worst of the competition during the first season. Bulbs of the simpler more attractive forms of narcissi, lilies, snow-drops, grape hyacinths can all be naturalized by planting them directly into the existing turf. But they must be scattered at random and seem to have been growing there for ever.

Once they have matured, areas like this are among the loveliest of gardens.

G.R.

*Secret Gardens
and Sunken Gardens*

GIARDINO SEGRETO

Into a little close of mine I went,
  One morning when the sun with his fresh light
  Was rising all refulgent and unshent.
Rose-trees are planted there in order bright.
  Whereto I turned charmed eyes, and long did stay,
  Taking my fill of that new-found delight.
Red and white roses bloomed upon the spray;
  One opened, leaf by leaf, to greet the morn,
Shyly, at first, then in sweet disarray;
Another, yet a youngling, newly born,
  Scarce struggled from the bud, and there were some
  Whose petals closed them from the air forlorn;
Another fell, and showered the grass with bloom;
  Thus I behold the roses dawn and die,
  And one short hour their loveliness consume . . .

LORENZO THE MAGNIFICENT

THE SECRET GARDEN

This hiding place so dear unto myself,
And, pray and believe so full itself of charm,
Will keep me here for you in safe retreat
Through all September's unsalubrious hours.

HORACE

TO VITA

8 June, 1937
Never has Sissinghurst looked more lovely or been
more appreciated. I must say, Farley has made the place

look like a gentleman's garden, and you with your extraordinary taste have made it look like nobody's garden but your own. I think the secret of your gardening is simply that you have the courage to abolish ugly or unsuccessful flowers. Except for those beastly red-hot pokers which you have a weakness for, there is not an ugly flower in the whole place. Then I think, si j'ose m'exprimer ainsi that the design is really rather good. I mean we have got what we wanted to get – a perfect proportion between the classic and the romantic, between the element of expectation and the element of surprise. Thus the main axes are terminated in a way to satisfy expectation, yet they are in themselves so tricky that they also cause surprise. But the point of the garden will not be apparent until the hedges have grown up, especially (most important of all) the holly hedge in the flower garden. But it is lovely, lovely, lovely – and you must be pleased with your work.

HAROLD NICOLSON

SUDDENLY A GARDEN

The back side of the house was neither field, garden, nor orchard; or, rather, it was both field, garden, and orchard: for as soon as the descending of the stairs had delivered them down, they came into a place cunningly set with trees of the most taste-pleasing fruits; but scarcely they had taken that into their consideration, but that they were suddenly stept into a delicate Green; of each side of the Green a Thicket, and behind the Thickets again new Beds of Flowers, which being under the Trees were to them a Pavilion, and they to the Trees a Mosaical floor; so that it seemed that Art therein would needs be delightful, by counterfeiting his enemy Error, and making order in confusion.

SIR PHILIP SIDNEY

THE SUNKEN GARDEN*

Speak not—whisper not;
Here bloweth thyme and bergamot;
Softly on the evening hour,
Secret herbs their spices shower,
Dark-spiked rosemary and myrrh,
Lean-stalked, purple lavender;
Hides within her bosom, too,
All her sorrows, bitter rue.

Breathe not—trespass not;
Of this green and darkling spot,
Latticed from the moon's beams,
Perchance a distant dreamer dreams;
Perchance upon its darkening air,
The unseen ghosts of children fare,
Faintly swinging, sway and sweep,
Like lovely sea-flowers in its deep;
While, unmoved, to watch and ward,
'Mid its gloom'd and daisied sward,
Stands with bowed and dewy head
That one little leaden Lad.

WALTER DE LA MARE

*This was the most popular single entry in the *Sunday Times* competition

MOLTO BELLO

'My secret little garden,' continued Miss Mapp as they came to the archway. 'When I am in here and shut the door, I mustn't be disturbed for anything less than a telegram. A rule of the house: I am very strict about it. The tower of the church keeping watch, as I always say, over my little nook, and taking care of me. Otherwise not overlooked at all. A little paved walk round it, you see, flower-beds, a pocket-handkerchief of a lawn, and in the middle a pillar with a bust of good Queen Anne. Picked it up in a shop here for a song. One of my lucky days.'

'Oh Georgie, isn't it too sweet?' cried Lucia. 'Un giardino segreto. Molto bello!'

E.F. BENSON

HOW STILL!

She was standing *inside* the secret garden.

It was the sweetest, most mysterious-looking place anyone could imagine. The high walls which shut it in were covered with the leafless stems of climbing roses, which were so thick that they were matted together. Mary Lennox knew they were roses because she had seen a great many roses in India. All the ground was covered with grass of a wintry brown, and out of it grew clumps of bushes which were surely rose-bushes if they were alive. There were numbers of standard roses which had so spread their branches that they were like little trees. There were other trees in the garden, and one of the things that made the place look strangest and loveliest was that climbing roses had run all over them and swung down long tendrils which made light swaying curtains, and here and there they had caught at each other or at a far-reaching branch and had crept from one tree to another and made lovely bridges of themselves. There were neither leaves nor roses on them now, and Mary did not know whether they were dead or alive, but their thin grey or brown branches and sprays looked like a sort of hazy mantle spreading over everything, walls, and trees, and even brown grass, where they had fallen from their fastenings and run along the ground. It was this hazy tangle from tree to tree which made it look so mysterious. Mary had thought it must be different from other gardens which had not been left all by themselves so long; and, indeed, it was different from any other place she had ever seen in her life.

'How still it is!' she whispered. 'How still!'

FRANCES HODGSON BURNETT

A GARDEN ENCLOSED

The Bridegroom
She is a garden enclosed,
my sister, my promised bride;
a garden enclosed,
a sealed fountain.

Your shoots form an orchard of
        pomegranate trees,
the rarest essences are yours:
nard and saffron,
calamus and cinnamon,
with all the incense-bearing trees;
myrrh and aloes,
with the subtlest odours.

Fountain that makes the gardens fertile,
well of living water,
streams flowing down from Lebanon.

The Bride

Awake, north wind,
come, wind of the south!
Breathe over my garden,
to spread its sweet smell around.
Let my Beloved come into his garden,
let him taste its rarest fruits.

The Bridegroom

I come into the garden,
my sister, my promised bride,
I gather my myrrh and balsam,
I eat my honey and my honeycomb,
I drink my wine and my milk.
Eat, friends, and drink,
drink deep, my dearest friends.

SONG OF SONGS 4:12–5:1

SECRET

Most Renaissance gardens had their secret area (*giardino segreto*) but in modern times among the greatest of exponents of the concept was that strange pair of gardeners Harold Nicolson and Vita Sackville-West. Nicolson was a diplomat, turned journalist, turned politician, and Vita was a complex and exotic creature. Together the Nicolsons lived a life divided into many curious compartments, and a psychiatrist might predicate that this is why their garden had to become a series of secret places.

'Secret' areas in a garden are necessary not for discreet encounters but to supply the vital element of surprise for everyone who walks or works in it. Even the most spectacular landscapes can pall if all their features are too evident. The half-seen or partially envisaged has more charm than the overt. And sometimes in a frenetic world a sensation of privacy can be therapeutic. It can be achieved quite simply – for example a seat placed in an unexpected alcove can have great effect. A thick, tall evergreen hedge planted far enough in from the lateral boundaries of a garden wall, when it has matured, allows the removal of one or two of the original plants to provide a sheltered haven in which to sit.

Gardeners with irregularly shaped plots are frequently at an advantage, particularly if their land forms an 'L', because clever planting can deceive the eye into imagining that the garden is a simple rectangle of almost limitless depth. Some attractive feature – a particularly decorative shrub or a masonry artefact – can be used to lure visitors down the garden and they will be surprised when they realize that it continues round the corner to the right or left. And the theatre designers' ploy of obtaining a sense of depth by arranging for fairly obvious features to emerge from the margins of the scene in the fore and middle ground can easily be copied by gardeners when planting shrubs and trees. The area beyond these partial screens could be used to locate secret areas.

Imagine a conventional house with a boring stretch of lawn behind. Surprise can be achieved by placing a thick hedge, wall or well-clad trellis running across the garden near its far boundary, with a narrow gap through it which the eye can just penetrate. The lawn in front of this barrier could be continued as a path running through the gap so that, standing near the house, the imagination would conceive that there was a lawn at the far side. In fact, apart from the central path of lawn, the rest of that area could be a formal sunken paved garden, quite different in spirit from the lawn.

G.R.

*Scented and
Shaded Gardens
and Moonlight*

I SMELT A GARDIN

Comming to kisse her lyps (such grace I found)
   Me seemed I smelt a gardin of sweet flowres,
That dainty odours from them threw around
   For damzels fit to decke their lovers' bowres.
Her lips did smell lyke unto Gillyflowers,
   Her ruddy cheekes like unto Roses red,
Her snowy browes lyke budded Bellamoures,
   Her lovely eyes lyke Pincks but newly spred;
Her goodly bosome like a Strawberry bed,
   Her neck lyke to a bounch of Cullambynes,
Her brest lyke lillyes ere theyr leaves be shed,
   Her nipples lyke yong blossomed Jessemynes.
      Such fragrant flowres doe give most odorous
         smell;
      But her sweet odour did them all excell.

EDMUND SPENSER

THE BREATH OF FLOWERS IS SWEET

And because the breath of flowers is far sweeter in the air (where it comes and goes, like the warbling of music) than in the hand, therefore nothing is more fit for that delight, than to know what be the flowers and plants that do best perfume the air. Roses, damask and red, are fast flowers of their smells; so that you may walk by a whole row of them, and find nothing of their sweetness; yea, though it be in a morning's dew. Bays likewise yield no smell as they grow. Rosemary little; nor sweet marjoram. That which above all others yields the sweetest smell in the air, is the violet; specially the white double violet, which comes twice a year; about the middle of April, and about Bartholomewtide. Next to that is the musk-rose. Then the strawberry-leaves dying, which [yield] a most excellent cordial smell. Then the flower of the vines; it is a little dust, like the dust of a bent, which grows upon the cluster in the first coming forth. Then sweet-briar. Then wall-flowers, which are very delightful to be set under a parlour or lower chamber window. Then pinks and gillyflowers, specially the matted pink and clove gillyflower. Then the flower of the lime-tree. Then the honeysuckles, so they be somewhat afar off. Of bean flowers I speak not, because they are field flowers. But those which perfume the air most delightfully, not passed by as the rest, but being trodden upon and crushed, are three: that is, burnet, wild thyme, and water-mints. Therefore you are to set whole alleys of them, to have the pleasure when you walk or tread.

FRANCIS BACON

CEREUS

Children of night! unfolding meekly, slowly
To the sweet breathings of the shadowy hours,
When dark blue heavens look softest and most holy,
And glow-worm light is in the forest bowers;
    To solemn things and deep,
    To spirit-haunted sleep,
    To thoughts, all purified
    From earth, ye seem allied;
      O dedicated flowers!

FELICIA DOROTHEA HEMANS

THE PLEASANT ODOUR OF THE ORCHARD

Chiefly the Pleasure this sense meets with is from the
sweet smelling blossomes of all the fruit trees, which
from the time of their breaking forth, till their fall,
breathe out a most pretious and pleasant odour;
perfuming the aire throughout all the Orchard.

RALPH AUSTEN

YUCCA BY MOONLIGHT

Not long ago I was at a stately place in Shropshire, and
at the end of a broad walk, where a circle of yuccas had
been planted, there were no less than five in full flower,
throwing up pale jets of blossom, like fountains, towards
the sky. I never saw anything more perfect in its way.
But it is said that the right time to see a yucca is by
moonlight. There is a very striking passage in one of the
letters of the most remarkable of American women,
Margaret Fuller (afterwards Countess D'Ossoli), in
which she says:

'This flower' (it was the *Yucca filamentosa*) 'was
made for the moon as the Heliotrope is for the sun, and
refuses other influences, or to display her beauty in any
other light. Many white flowers are far more beautiful
by day. The lily, for instance, needs the broadest light to
manifest its purity, but these transparent leaves of
greenish white, which look dull in the day, are melted by
the moon to glistening silver . . .'

The second evening I went out into the garden
again. In clearest moonlight stood my flower, more
beautiful than ever. The stalk pierced the air like a
spear; all the little bells had erected themselves around

it in a most graceful array, with petals more transparent than silver, and of softer light than the diamond. Their edges were clearly but not sharply defined—they seemed to have been made by the moon's rays. The leaves, which had looked ragged by day, now seemed fringed by most delicate gossamer, and the plant might claim, with pride, its distinctive epithet of *filamentosa*.

HENRY BRIGHT

ALL TO SWEETNESS TURNS

To-day I think
Only with scents,—scents dead leaves yield,
And bracken, and wild carrot's seed,
And the square mustard field;

Odours that rise
When the spade wounds the root of tree,
Rose, currant, raspberry, or goutweed,
Rhubarb or celery;

The smoke's smell, too,
Flowing from where a bonfire burns
The dead, the waste, the dangerous,
And all to sweetness turns . . .

EDWARD THOMAS

PARFUMS FRAIS

Il est des parfums frais comme des chairs d'enfants,
Doux comme les hautbois, verts comme les prairies,
—Et d'autres, corrompus, riches et triumphants,

Ayant l'expansion des choses infinies,
Comme l'ambre, le musc, le benjoin et l'encens,
Qui chantent les transports de l'esprit et des sens.

CHARLES BAUDELAIRE

THE GREAT GATSBY'S GARDEN

There was music from my neighbour's house through
the summer nights. In his blue gardens, men and girls
came and went like moths among the whisperings and
the champagne and the stars.

F. SCOTT FITZGERALD

DARK SHADOW

Like some young cypress, tall, and dark, and straight,
Which in a queen's secluded garden throws
Its slight dark shadow on the moonlit turf,
By midnight, to a bubbling fountain's sound –

MATTHEW ARNOLD

SCENT AND THE LOVER

. . . O would to God (so I might have my fee)
My lips were honey, and thy mouth a bee.

Then should'st thou suck my sweet and my fair flower
That now is ripe, and full of honey-berries:
Then would I lead thee to my pleasant bower

Filled full of grapes, of mulberries, and cherries;
   Then should'st thou be my wasp or else my bee,
   I would thy hive, and thou my honey be.

And in the sweltering heat of summer time,
I would make cabinets for thee (my love:)
Sweet-smelling arbours made of eglantine
Should be thy shrine, and I would be thy dove.
   Cool cabinets of fresh green laurel boughs
   Should shadow us, o'er-set with thick-set yews.

Nay more than this, I have a garden-plot,
Wherein there wants nor herbs, nor roots, nor flowers;
(Flowers to smell, roots to eat, herbs for the pot,)
And dainty shelters when the welkin lowers:
   Sweet-smelling beds of lillies and of roses,
   Which rosemary banks and lavender incloses.

There grows the gillyflower, the mind, the daisy
(Both red and white,) the blue-veined-violet:
The purple hyacinth, the spike to please thee,
The scarlet dyed carnation bleeding yet;
   The sage, the savory, and sweet marjoram,
   Isop, thyme, and eye-bright, good for the blind and
      dumb.

The pink, the primrose, cowslip, and daffadilly,
The hare-bell blue, the crimson columbine,
Sage, lettuce, parsley, and the milk-white lilly,
The rose, and speckled flower called sops-in-wine,
   Fine pretty king-cups, and the yellow boots,
   That grows by rivers, and by shallow brooks.

RICHARD BARNFIELD

SOME SCENTS OVERPOWER

The flowers of the evergreen magnolia, and those of the orange, have an oppressive fragrance, as have those of the heliotrope and the tuberose . . .

JANE LOUDON

Our ginger plant is now in magnificent blossom, a curious tendrilled flower like an orchis, and the scent so strong that we have been obliged to turn the plant from the dining into the drawing room and thence into the hall.

REV. FRANCIS KILVERT

THE SPICES ARE WAFTED

Come into the garden, Maud,
  For the black bat, night, has flown,
Come into the garden, Maud,
  I am here at the gate alone;
And the woodbine spices are wafted abroad,
  And the musk of the rose is blown.

For a breeze of morning moves,
  And the planet of Love is on high,
Beginning to faint in the light that she loves
  On a bed of daffodil sky,
To faint in the light of the sun she loves,
  To faint in his light, and to die.

ALFRED TENNYSON

MOONLIGHT NIGHTS

Often, on moonlight nights in spring, the solitary fork of some one who had not been able to tear himself away would be heard and the scent of his twitch fire smoke would float in at the windows. It was pleasant, too, in summer twilight, perhaps in hot weather when water was scarce, to hear the swish of water on parched earth in a garden – water which had been fetched from the brook a quarter of a mile distant.

FLORA THOMPSON

SILVER

Slowly, silently, now the moon
Walks the night in her silver shoon;
This way, and that, she peers, and sees
Silver fruit upon silver trees;
One by one the casements catch
Her beams beneath the silvery thatch;
Couched in his kennel, like a log,
With paws of silver sleeps the dog;
From their shadowy cote the white breasts peep
Of doves in a silver-feathered sleep;
A harvest mouse goes scampering by,
With silver claws, and silver eye;
And moveless fish in the water gleam,
By silver reeds in a silver stream.

WALTER DE LA MARE

FINE MOONSHINE

It being a very fine moonshine, my wife and Mercer came into the garden, and, my business being done, we sang till about twelve at night, with mighty pleasure to ourselves and neighbours, by their casements opening.

SAMUEL PEPYS

SCENTED GARDEN

A garden which did not offer a palette of fragrances during most of the year would be considered a failure. Fortunately such a situation rarely prevails. Even soil wet by showers or leaf mould offer their own pleasing scents. And when summer arrives most richly planted established gardens are sufficiently permeated by delicious odours to excite even those with the dullest sense of smell.

The greatest challenge for gardeners is to ensure that their garden is rich in perfume during the winter months when there is little warmth to evaporate the essential oils which tickle our perceptions. There are several shrubs which are well worth including in any temperate zone garden because they have this capacity to please even when the weather is at its bleakest. Among the best are *Abelia chinensis* – vanilla-scented, *Chimonanthus fragrans* – violet-scented, two *Daphnes* – *mezereum* – violet-scented and *odora* – spicy-scented, *Hamamelis mollis* – very sweetly scented, two *Loniceras* – *fragrantissima* and *purpurii* – both honey-scented, *Mahonia japonica* – like Lily of the Valley, *Sarcococcus ruscifolia* – with a fruity aroma, *Viburnum bodnantense* – sweet-scented and *Viburnum foetidum* – redolent of jonquils.

In the evening after a scorching day, we are most likely to wander slowly round the garden and that's a time when we appreciate most the perfume of the plants. To help nature along, plant specifically night-scented flowers at strategic places in the garden. Among the best are: *Hesperis fragrans* – clove-scented, *Linnaea borealis* – honeysuckle-scented, *Myosotis macrantha* – softly perfumed, *Nicotiana affinis* – sweetly scented, *Oenothera biennis* – sweetly scented, *Silene noctiflora* – carnation-scented, *Sisyrinchium odoratissimum* with a heavy exotic perfume.

G.R.

Rose Gardens

ROSES AND ROZIZ

And after all the weather was ideal. They could not have had a more perfect day for a garden party if they had ordered it. Windless, warm, the sky without a cloud. Only the blue was veiled with a haze of light gold, as it is sometimes in early summer. The gardener had been up since dawn, mowing the lawns and sweeping them, until the grass and the dark flat rosettes where the daisy plants had been seemed to shine. As for the roses, you could not help feeling they understood that roses are the only flowers that impress people at garden parties; the only flowers that anybody is certain of knowing. Hundreds, yes, literally hundreds had come out in a single night; the green bushes bowed down as though they had been visited by archangels.

KATHERINE MANSFIELD

And this is certain; if so be
You could just now my garden see,
The aspic of my flowers so bright
Would make you shudder with delight.

And if you voz to see my roziz
As is a boon to all men's noziz, –
You'd fall upon your back and scream –
'O Lawk! O criky! it's a dream!'

EDWARD LEAR

THE ROSE SPEAKS

In this solemn randevoux of flowers and herbs, the Rose stood forth, and made an oration to this effect.

It is not unknown to you, how I have precedency of all flowers, confirmed unto me under the patent of a double sence, sight and smell. What more curious colours? how do all diers blush, when they behold my blushing as conscious to themselves that their art cannot imitate that tincture, which nature hath stamped upon me. Smell, it is not lusciously offensive, nor dangerously faint, but comforteth with a delight, and delighteth with the comfort thereof: yea, when dead, I am more soveraigne than living: what cordials are made of my syrups? how many corrupted lungs (those fans of nature) sore wasted with consumption that they seem utterly unable any longer to cool the heat of the heart, with their ventilation, are with conserves made of my stamped leaves, restored to their former soundness again. More would I say in my own cause, but that happily I may be taxed of pride, and selfe-flattery, who speake much in mine own behalf, and therefore I leave the rest to the judgement of such as hear me, and pass from this discourse to my just complaint.

There is lately a flower (shall I call it so? in courtesie I will tearme it so, though it deserve not the appellation) a Toolip, which hath engrafted the love and affections of most people unto it; and what is this Toolip? a well complexion'd stink, an ill favour wrapt up in pleasant colours; as for the use thereof in physick, no physitian hath honoured it yet with the mention, nor with a Greek, or Latin name, so inconsiderable hath it hitherto been accompted; and yet this is that which filleth all gardens, hundred of pounds being given for the root

thereof, whilst I the Rose, am neglected and con-
temned, and conceived beneath the honour of noble
hands, and fit only to grow in the gardens of yeomen.

THOMAS FULLER

A PERSIAN GARDEN

On my first entering this bower of fairyland (indeed I
may call it the very garden of Beauty and the Beast!) I
was struck with the appearance of two rose-trees, full
fourteen feet high, laden with thousands of flowers, in
every degree of expansion, and of a bloom and delicacy
of scent, that imbued the whole atmosphere with the
most exquisite perfume. Indeed, I believe that in no
country of the world does the rose grow in such
perfection as in Persia: in no country is it so cultivated,
and prized by the natives. Their gardens and courts are
crowded with its plants, their rooms ornamented with
vases, filled with its gathered bunches, and every bath
strewed with the full-blown flowers, plucked from the
ever-replenished stems. Even the humblest individual,
who pays a piece of copper money for a few whiffs of a
kalion, feels a double enjoyment when he finds it stuck
with a bud from his dear native tree! But in this
delicious garden of Negauristan, the eye and the smell
were not the only senses regaled by the presence of
roses. The ear was enchanted by the wild and beautiful
notes of nightingales, whose warblings seem to increase
in melody and softness, with the unfolding of their
favourite flowers; verifying the song of their poet, who
says: 'When the roses fade, when the charms of the
bower are passed away, the fond tale of the nightingale
no longer animates the scene.'

SIR ROBERT KER PORTER

CLIMBING ROSES

So, if it is to be a rose-garden, do not choose those stunted, unnatural earth-loving strains, which have nothing of vigour and wildness in them, nor banish other flowers which may do homage to the beauty of a rose as courtiers to a queen. Let climbing roses drop in a veil from the terrace and smother with flower-spangled embroidery the garden walls, run riot over vaulted arcades, clamber up lofty obelisks of leaf-tangled trellis, twine themselves round the pillars of a rose-roofed temple, where little avalanches of sweetness shall rustle down at a touch and the dusty gold of the sunshine shall mingle with the summer snow of the flying petals. Let them leap in a great bow or fall in a creamy cataract to a foaming pool of flowers. In the midst of the garden set a statue of Venus with a great bloom trained to her hand, or of Flora, her cornucopia overflowing with white rosettes, or a tiny basin where leaden *amorini* seated upon the margin are fishing with trailing buds.

SIR GEORGE SITWELL

RUBAIYAT OF OMAR KHAYYAM

I sometimes think that never blows so red
The Rose as where some buried Caesar bled;
That every Hyacinth the Garden wears
Dropt in its lap from some once lovely Head.

And this delightful Herb whose tender Green
Fledges the River's Lip on which we lean –
Ah, lean upon it lightly! for who knows

From what once Lovely Lip it springs unseen.

(TRANSLATED BY) FITZGERALD

AND THE ROSES – THE ROSES!

They always called it Magic, and indeed it seemed like it in the months that followed – the wonderful months – the radiant months – the amazing ones. Oh! the things which happened in that garden! If you have never had a garden, you cannot understand, and if you have had a garden, you will know that it would take a whole book to describe all that came to pass there. At first it seemed that green things would never cease pushing their way through the earth, in the grass, in the beds, even in the crevices of the walls. Then the green things began to show buds, and the buds began to unfurl and show colour, every shade of blue, every shade of purple, every tint and hue of crimson. In its happy days flowers had been tucked away into every inch and hole and corner. Ben Weatherstaff had seen it done and had himself scraped out mortar from between the bricks of the wall and made pockets of earth for lovely clinging things to grow on. Iris and white lilies rose out of the grass in sheaves, and the green alcoves filled themselves with amazing armies of the blue and white flower lances of tall delphiniums or columbines or campanulas.

'She was main fond o' them – she was,' Ben Weatherstaff said. 'She liked them things as was allus pointin' up to th' blue sky, she used to tell. Not as she was once o' them as looked down on th' earth – not her. She just loved it, but she said as th' blue sky allus looked so joyful.'

The seeds Dickon and Mary had planted grew as if

fairies had tended them. Satiny poppies of all tints danced in the breeze by the score, gaily defying flowers which had lived in the garden for years, and which it might be confessed seemed rather to wonder how such new people had got there. And the roses – the roses! Rising out of the grass, tangled round the sun-dial, wreathing the tree-trunks, and spreading over them with long garlands falling in cascades – they came alive day by day, hour by hour. Fair, fresh leaves, and buds – and buds – tiny at first, but swelling and working Magic until they burst and uncurled into cups of scent delicately spilling themselves over their brims and filling the garden air.

FRANCES HODGSON BURNETT

ROSES

Unless they are large-scaled and wonderfully maintained, formal rosebeds have no real place in the modern garden. From November through to April their heavily pruned bare stems sticking out from a thick mattress of rotted horse manure like amputated limbs have little appeal.

In summer the scentless waxy perfection which most breeders have given their blooms can be stultifying. It's little wonder that many of the world's rose breeders have found their market beginning to dwindle as gardeners turn to more satisfying plants. And that's a pity when the rose used to be, and could again become, the gardener's emblem.

Happily it's not too late for the situation to be changed. Some far-sighted breeders and growers have striven to liberate the rose; freeing it from the constraints of the formal bed. Realizing that in these days of low maintenance gardening there would be a market for roses which would look after themselves and could be treated like any other shrub growing out of a lawn, meadow lawn or shrubbery, at least one breeder has crossed old varieties of shrub rose with modern hybrid roses. This has produced new shrub roses with all the good characteristics of beautiful free flowers, heavy perfume and ruggedness of the old, coupled with the recurrent flowering ability of the modern hybrids.

Shrub roses hardly need pruning, and are very vigorous and do need a largish garden to accommodate them satisfactorily.

The cramped nature of many modern gardens influenced the programmes of other breeders too. The result has been a large range of miniature or at least much more compact roses which can be grown alongside herbaceous plants in the mixed herbaceous and shrub borders which have become so popular now that help in the garden is so difficult to find and so expensive.

The popularity of ground cover plants which stifle weeds in areas of a garden which are inaccessible, or where the gardener is reluctant to work, has led rose breeders to produce low growing rambling roses for this purpose. So the charm of the rose can be reintroduced to the garden without the effort which they formerly required.

G.R.

*Water Gardens
and Fountains*

VILLA D'ESTE GARDENS

'Of course you saw the Villa d'Este Gardens,'
Writes one of my Italianistic friends.
Of course; of course; I saw them in October,
Spired with pinaceous ornamental gloom
Of that arboreal elegy the cypress.

These fountains, too, 'like ghosts of cypresses'; –
(The phrase occurred to me whilst I was leaning
On an old balustrade; imbibing sunset;
Wrapped in my verse vocation) – how they linked me
With Byron, Landor, Liszt and Robert Browning.

Their Browning jogged my elbow; bade me hob nob
With some forgotten painter of dim frescoes
That haunt the Villa's intramural twilight.
(While roaming in the Villa d'Este Gardens
I felt like that . . . and fumbled for my notebook)

SIEGFRIED SASSOON

OF FOUNTAINS

For fountains, they are a great beauty and refreshment;
but pools mar all, and make the garden unwholesome
and full of flies and frogs. Fountains I intend to be of
two natures: the one, that sprinkleth or spouteth water;
the other, a fair receipt of water, of some thirty or forty
foot square, but without fish, or slime, or mud. For the
first, the ornaments of images gilt, or of marble, which
are in use, do well: but the main matter is, so to convey
the water, as it never stay, either in the bowls or in the
cistern; that the water be never by rest discoloured,

green or red or the like, or gather any mossiness or putrefaction. Besides that, it is to be cleansed every day by the hand. Also some steps up to it, and some fine pavement about it, doth well. As for the other kind of fountain, which we may call a bathing pool, it may admit much curiosity and beauty, wherewith we will not trouble ourselves: as, that the bottom be finely paved, and with images; the sides likewise; and withal embellished with coloured glass, and such things of lustre; encompassed also with fine rails of low statues. But the main point is the same which we mentioned in the former kind of fountain; which is, that the water be in perpetual motion, fed by a water higher than the pool, and delivered into it by fair spouts, and then discharged away under ground, by some equality of bores, that it stay little. And for fine devices, of arching water without spilling, and making it rise in several forms (of feathers, drinking glasses, canopies, and the like), they be pretty things to look on, but nothing to health and sweetness.

FRANCIS BACON

SPRINGS OF WATER
FROM THE STONE

A Wat'ry Heap by a fresh Torrent fed,
Hoary with Froth, lifts up its reverend Head,
Whence various Currents falling, their Recoyl
Makes them, when cold as Ice, appear to boyl.

Out from his Temples in an artful Crown
Clear Drops like strings of Pearls, come trickling
    down,

Which quickly caught, and thence dispers'd again,
Seem like a Cloud burst into Showres of Rain.

As once Enceladus, our Architect
Great Heaps on Heaps of Marble does erect;
And, like a second Moses, when that's done,
Commands fresh Springs of Water from the Stone.

When Heav'ns are clear, this Man a second Jove,
From Earth exhales the Waters up above,
And thence in Cataracts can make them pour
When in the Sky there's neither Cloud nor Showre.

PHILLIP AYRES

A FRENCH VIEW

The music of the organ, which is real music and a natural organ, though always playing the same thing, is effected by means of the water, which falls with great violence into a round arched cave and agitates the air that is in there and from it through the pipes of the organ and supplies it with wind. Another stream of water, driving a wheel with certain teeth on it, causes the organ keyboard to be struck in a certain order; so you hear the song of birds, which are little bronze flutes that you see at regals; they give a sound like those little earthenware pots full of water that little children blow into by the spout, this by an artifice like that of the organ; and then by other springs they set in motion an owl, which, appearing at the top of the rock, makes his harmony cease instantly, for the birds are frightened by his presence; and then he leaves the place to them again. This goes on alternately as long as you want.

Elsewhere there issues a noise as of cannon shots. This is done by a sudden fall of water into channels; and the air, labouring at the same time to get out, engenders this noise. All these inventions, or similar ones, produced by these same natural causes, I have seen elsewhere.

There are ponds or reservoirs, with a stone margin all around and many tall freestone pillars above this parapet, about four paces apart from each other. From the head of these pillars water comes out with a great force, not upward, but towards the pond. The mouths, being thus turned inward and facing one another, cast and scatter the water into this pond with such force that these shafts of water come to meet and clash in the air, and produce a thick and continual rain falling in to the pond.

MONTAIGNE

A PERSIAN SWIMMING POOL

The place of greatest attraction to an oriental taste, certainly was the summer-bath. It seemed to comprise everything of seclusion, elegance, and that luxurious enjoyment, which has too often been the chief occupation of some Asiatic princes; and perhaps will ever be the favourite recreation with them all. This bath-saloon, or court (for it is difficult to give it an exactly appropriate name), is circular, with a vast basin in its centre, of pure white marble, of the same shape, and about sixty or seventy feet in diameter. This is filled with the clearest water, sparkling in the sun, for its only canopy is the vault of heaven; but rose-trees, with other pendant shrubs bearing flowers, cluster near it; and, at times, their waving branches throw a beautifully quivering shade over the excessive brightness of the water. Round the sides of the court, are two ranges, one above the other, of little chambers, looking towards the bath, and furnished with every refinement of the harem. These are for the accommodation of the ladies, who accompany the Shah during his occasional sojourns at the Negauristan. They undress or repose in these, before or after the delight of bathing; for so fond are they of this luxury, they remain in the water for hours; and sometimes, when the heat is very relaxing, come out more dead than alive.

SIR ROBERT KER PORTER

MONET: LES NYMPHEAS

... These lilies, if these things are water lilies
Which are dancers growing dim across no floor;
These mayflies; whirled duet orbiting in the sun;
This blossoming, diffused as rushlights; galactic
    vapours ...

W.D. SNODGRASS

AN ARTIFICIAL WATERFALL

There were various compartments, the connexion of which was well managed, and although the whole ground did not exceed five or six acres, it was so much varied as to seem four times larger. The space contained close alleys and open walks; a very pretty artificial waterfall; a fountain also, consisting of a considerable jet-d'eau, whose streams glittered in the sunbeams, and exhibited a continual rainbow. There was a cabinet of verdure as the French call it, to cool the summer heat, and there was a terrace sheltered from the north-east by a noble holly hedge, with all its glittering spears, where you might have the full advantage of the sun in the clear frosty days of winter . . .

SIR WALTER SCOTT

THE EMPEROR'S GARDEN NEAR PEKING

All the Risings and Hills are sprinkled with Trees; and particularly with Flowering-trees, which are here very common. The Sides of the Canals, or lesser Streams, are not faced, (as they are with us), with smooth Stone, and in a strait Line; but look rude and rustic, with different Pieces of Rock, some of which jut out, and others recede inwards; and are placed with so much Art, that you would take it to be the Work of Nature. In some Parts the Water is wide, in others narrow; here it serpentizes, and there spreads away, as if it was really push'd off by the Hills and Rocks. The Banks are sprinkled with Flowers; which rise up even thro' the Hollows in the Rock-work, as if they had been produced there naturally. They have a great Variety of them, for every Season of the Year.

Beyond these Streams there are always Walks, or rather, Paths, pav'd with small Stones; which lead from one Valley to another. These Paths too are irregular; and sometimes wind along the Banks of the Water, and at others run out wide from them . . .

I have already told you, that these little Streams, or Rivers, are carried on to supply several larger Pieces of Water, and Lakes. One of these Lakes is very near Five

Miles round; and they call it a Meer, or Sea. This is one of the most beautiful Parts in the whole Pleasure-ground. On the Banks, are several Pieces of Building separated from each other by the Rivulets, and artificial Hills above mentioned . . .

The Banks of this charming Water are infinitely varied: there are no two Parts of it alike. Here you see Keys of smooth Stone; with Porticoes, Walks, and Paths, running down to them from the Palaces that surround the Lake; there, others of Rock-work; that fall into Steps, contrived with the greatest Art that can be conceived: here, natural Terraces with winding Steps at each End, to go up to the Palaces that are built upon them; and above these, other Terraces, and other Palaces, that rise higher and higher, and form a sort of Amphitheatre. There again a Grove of Flowering-trees presents itself to your Eye; and a little farther, you see a Spread of wild Forest-trees, and such as grow only on the most barren Mountains: then, perhaps, vast Timber-trees with their Under-wood; then, Trees from all foreign Countries; and then, some all blooming with Flowers, and others all laden with Fruits of different Kinds.

FATHER ATTIRET

FISH POND

The scullery maid, before the plates came out, was cooling her cheeks by the lily pond. There had always been lilies there, self-sown from wind-dropped seed, floating red and white on the green plates of their leaves. Water, for hundreds of years, had silted down into the hollow, and lay there four or five feet deep over a black cushion of mud. Under the thick plate of green water, glazed in their self-centred world, fish swam – gold, splashed with white, streaked with black or silver. Silently they manoeuvred in their water world, poised in the blue patch made by the sky, or shot silently to the edge where the grass, trembling, made a fringe of nodding shadow. On the water-pavement, spiders printed their delicate feet. A grain fell and spiralled down; a petal fell, filled and sank.

VIRGINIA WOOLF

OLD POND

Ahmed came to a halt and they meekly followed suit. He had stopped in front of a little circle of level ground, an old pond half smothered in young grass and potentilla in flower. Its crumbling stone rim could no longer keep back the invasion of marsh marigolds and poppies. A trickle of water, deserting its dried-up spout in the mouth of a stone lion's head, ran free between the broken flags.

'Oh,' cried Rose in delight.

'Rather snappy,' declared Odette. 'Bernard, what about something like that for a garden terrace at Auteuil?'

COLETTE

REMEMBRANCE OF WATER-LILIES – COMBRAY

But farther on the current slackened, where the stream ran through a property thrown open to the public by its owner, who had made a hobby of aquatic gardening, so that the little ponds into which the Vivonne was here diverted were aflower with water-lilies. As the banks at this point were thickly wooded, the heavy shade of the trees gave the water a background which was ordinarily dark green, although sometimes, when we were coming home on a dark evening after a stormy afternoon, I have seen in its depths a clear, crude blue that was almost violet, suggesting a floor of Japanese cloissonné. Here and there, on the surface, floated, blushing like a strawberry, the scarlet heart of a lily set in a ring of white petals.

Beyond these the flowers were more frequent, but paler, less glossy, more thickly seeded, more tightly folded, and disposed, by accident, in festoons so graceful that I would fancy I saw floating upon the stream, as though after the dreary stripping of the decorations used in some Watteau festival, moss-roses in loosened garlands. Elsewhere a corner seemed to be reserved for the commoner kinds of lily; of a neat pink or white like rocket-flowers, washed clean like porcelain, with housewifely care; while, a little farther again, were others, pressed close together in a floating garden-bed, as though pansies had flown out of a garden like butterflies and were hovering with blue and burnished wings over the transparent shadowiness of this watery border; this skiey border also, for it set beneath the flowers a soil of a colour more precious, more moving than their own; and both in the afternoon, when it sparkled beneath the lilies in the kaleidoscope of a happiness silent, restless, and alert, and towards evening, when it was filled like a distant haven with the roseate dreams of the setting sun, incessantly changing and ever remaining in harmony, about the more permanent colour of the flowers themselves, with the utmost profundity, evanescence, and mystery – with a quiet suggestion of infinity; afternoon or evening, it seemed to have set them flowering in the heart of the sky.

MARCEL PROUST

THE SOUL OF A GARDEN AT VITERBO

The Duke of Lante's garden is of another character, a place not of grandeur or tragedy but of enchanting loveliness, a paradise of gleaming water, gay flowers and golden light. The long, straight, dusty road from Viterbo leads at length by a bridge across a deep ravine to a gap in the town walls of Bagnaia, 'twixt Gothic castle and Baroco church, then turning at a right angle in the piazza one sees in front the great Renaissance gateway which opens into the garden. But it is better, if permission may be obtained, to enter the park, and striking upward by green lawns and ilex groves to follow from its source the tiny streamlet upon which pool, cascade, and water-temple are threaded like pearls upon a string. Dropping from a ferny grotto between two pillared loggias, this rivulet rises again in an elaborate fountain surrounded by mossy benches set in the alcoves of a low box hedge. Four giant plane-trees lift a canopy against the sun, and tall stone columns rising from a balustraded wall warn off the intruding woodland. Thence, running underground, it emerges unexpectedly in the centre of a broad flight of steps between the claws of a gigantic crab – Cardinal Gambara's cognisance – and races down a long scalloped trough, rippling and writhing like a huge snake over the carved shells which bar its passage. From this it drops over the edge of a small basin between two colossal river-gods into a pool below. The fall to the next level gives us a half-recessed "temple d'eau", with innumerable jets and runlets pouring from basin to basin; and here, flanked by stately plane-trees and by the two pavilions which make up the casino, is a grass plot commanding the loveliest view of the garden. Before us lies a square enclosure jutting out into the vale below, with high green hedges, sweet "broderies" of box bordered by flowers, and in the midst a broad water-garden leading by balustraded crossways to an island fountain which rises like a mount to four great figures of sombre-tinted stone. Water gushes from the points of the star which the naked athletes uplift, from the mouths of the lions by their side, from the masks on the balustrade, from the tiny galleys in which vagrant cupids are afloat upon the pools. It is a colour harmony of cool refreshing green and brighter flowers, of darkest bronze, blue pools and golden light. Much there is of mystery in the garden, of subtle magic, of strange, elusive charm which must be felt but cannot wholly be understood. Much, no doubt, depends upon the setting, upon the ancient ilexes and wild mountain flank, the mighty hedge of green at the further end with its great pillared gateway and the dark walls and orange-lichened roofs of the houses and tower irregularly grouped behind it; upon the quiet background, the opal hues of green, violet and grey in the softly modelled plain, and the shadowy outlines of the distant hills. But the soul of the garden is in the blue pools which, by some strange wizardry of the artist, to stair and terrace and window throw back the undimmed azure of the Italian sky.

OSBERT SITWELL

MIDMOST A FOUNTAIN

The garden, all walled about, coasted the palace. It had
about it and athwart the middle, spacious alleys, straight
as arrows and embowered with trellises of vines,
yielding a rare savor about the garden. The sides of
these alleys were walled with roses, red and white and
with jessamine. While the sun was highest one might go
all about neath odoriferous and delightsome shade.
Amiddleward the garden was a plat of very fine grass,
enamelled with a thousand kinds of flowers, closed
about with the greenest and lustiest of orange and citron
trees, the which, bearing at once old fruits and new, and
flowers, afforded the eyes a pleasant shade and were no
less grateful to the smell. Midmost the grass plat was a
fountain of whitest marble. From a figure that stood on
a column in its midst, sprang a great jet of water, high
towards the sky. With a delectable sound it fell back into
the wonder-limpid fountain. The water which over-
flowed the full basin issued forth by a hidden way,
encompassing the lawn by very goodly and curiously
wrought channels.

BOCCACCIO

GODDESS OF ABUNDANCE

The garden, like so many others in Sicily, was designed
on a level lower than the house, I think so that advantage
could be taken of a spring welling up there. It was very
large, and, when seen from a window of the house,
perfectly regular in its complicated system of alleys and
paths. It was all planted out with ilex and araucaria, the
alleys bordered with myrtle hedges; and in the furnace

of summer, when the jet of the spring dwindled, it was a paradise of parched scents of origan and catmint, as are so many gardens in Sicily that seem made to delight the nose rather than the eyes.

The long alleys surrounding it on all four sides were the only straight ones in the whole garden, for in the rest the designer had multiplied twists, turns, mazes and corridors, contributing to give it that tone of graceful mystery which enveloped the whole house. All these cross-alleys, however, came out eventually on to a big central clearing, the one where the spring had been found; this, now enclosed in an ornate prison, lightened with its spurts a great fountain in the centre of which, on an islet of artificial ruins, a dishevelled and ungirt goddess of Abundance poured torrents of water into a deep basin for ever crossed by friendly ripples. It was bounded by a balustrade, surmounted here and there by Tritons and Nereids sculptured in the act of diving with movements that were disordered in each individual statue but fused into a scenic whole. All round the fountain were stone benches darkened by centuries-old moss.

GIUSEPPE DI LAMPEDUSA

A VERSAILLES BASON

Arouse ye from your megrims and your melancholies, and (for exercise is good for you) throw away your night-cap, call for your jack-boots, and set out with me, for Versailles . . .

You descend a huge flight of steps in a semi-circle formed by woods, that are cut all around into niches, which are filled with beautiful copies of all the famous

antique statues in white marble. Just in the midst is the
bason of Latona; she and her children are standing on
the top of a rock in the middle, on the sides of which are
the peasants, some half, some totally changed into frogs,
all which throw out water at her in great plenty. From
this place runs on the great alley, which brings you into
a complete road, where is the bason of Apollo, the
biggest in the gardens. He is rising in his car out of the
water, surrounded by nymphs and tritons, all in bronze,
and finely executed, and these, as they play, raise a
perfect storm about him; beyond this is the great canal,
a prodigious long piece of water, that terminates the
whole, all this you have at one coup d'oeil in entering
the garden which is truly great.

THOMAS GRAY

IN PRAISE OF GARDENS

The desert about Tehran is renowned for the beauty of
its gardens. The Shah possesses several, others belong
to his sons, others to powerful ministers and wealthy
merchants. Sometimes across the gateways a chain is
drawn, denoting that the garden is Bast – sanctuary –
and into these the European may not go; but places of
refuge for the hunted criminal are, fortunately, few, and
generally the garden is open to all comers.

Perhaps the most beautiful of all is one which
belongs to the Shah, and which lies under a rocky
hillock crowned with the walls and towers of a palace.
We found ourselves at its gate one evening, after an
aimless canter across the desert, and determined to
enter. The loiterers in the gateway let us pass through
unchallenged. We crossed the little entrance-court and

came into a long dark avenue, fountains down the middle of it, and flower beds, in which the plants were pale and meagre for want of light; roses, the pink flowers which scent the rose-water, and briers, a froth of white and yellow bloom, growing along its edges in spite of the deep shade of the plane trees. Every tiny rill of water was fringed with violet leaves – you can imagine how in the spring the scent of the violets greets you out in the desert when you are still far away, like a hospitable friend coming open-armed down his steps to welcome you. We wandered along intersecting avenues, until we came to one broader than the rest, at the end of which stood a little house. Tiny streams flowed round and about it, flowed under its walls, and into its rooms; fountains splashed ceaselessly in front of it, a soft light wind swayed the heavy folds of the patterned curtains hanging half-way down across its deep balconies. The little dwelling looked like a fairy palace, jewelled with coloured tiles, unreal and fantastic, built half out of the ripple of water, and half out of the shadowy floating of its great curtains. Two or three steps and a narrow passage, and we were in the central room – such a room to lie and dream in through the hot summer days! – tiled with blue, in the middle an overflowing fountain, windows on either side opening down to the ground, the vaulted ceiling and the alcoved walls set with a mosaic of looking-glass, in whose diamonds and crescents the blue of the tiles and the spray of the tossing waters were reflected.

GERTRUDE BELL

NEARLY A TRAGEDY

When Shah Jahan was in Kashmir in 1633 he visited the
Nishat Bagh, then not a Royal Garden. Its high terraces
and wonderful views of the lakes and mountains so
delighted him that he at once decided that the gardens
were altogether too splendid for a subject, even though
that subject be his own Prime Minister, and father-in-
law. He told Asaf Khan on three occasions how much
he admired his pleasure garden, expecting that it would
be immediately offered for the Royal acceptance. But
the Prime Minister could not bring himself to surrender
his cherished pleasure, and remained silent. Then, as
now, the same stream supplied the Royal garden and
the Nishat Bagh, which lies on the mountain side
between Shalimar and the city of Srinagar. So Shah
Jahan in his anger ordered the water supply to be cut off
to the Nishat Bagh, and was avenged, for the garden he
envied was shorn of all its beauty.

Nothing is more desolate than one of these great
enclosures when their stone-lined tanks and water
channels are dry and empty. Asaf Khan, who was
staying in his summer palace at the time, could do
nothing, and all his household knew of his great and
bitter disappointment. One day, lost in a melancholy
reverie, he fell fast asleep in the shade by the empty
water course. At length a noise aroused him; rubbing
his eyes he could hardly believe what he saw, for the
fountains were all playing merrily once more, and the
long carved water chutes were white with foam. A
faithful servant, risking his life, had defied the Emper-
or's orders, and removed the obstruction from the
stream. Asaf Khan rebuked him for his zeal, and hastily
had the stream closed again. But the news reached the

Emperor in his garden at Shalimar, whereupon he sent for the terrified servant, and much to the surprise of the court, instead of punishing him, bestowed a robe of honour upon him to mark his admiration of his act of devoted service, at the same time granting a sanad, which gave the right to his master to draw water for his garden from the Shalimar stream.

MRS VILLIERS STUART

THE FOUNTAIN

And in the midst of all, a fountaine stood,
 Of richest substaunce, that on earth might bee,
 So pure and shiny, that the silver flood
 Through every channel running one might see;
 Mostly goodly it with curious imagerie
 Was over-wrought, and shapes of naked boyes,
 Of which some seem'd with lusty iollitee,
 To fly about, playing their wanton toyes,
Whilest others did them selves embay in liquid ioyes.

And over all, of purest gold was spred
 A teazle of yvie in his native hew:
 For the rich metall was so coloured,
 That wight, who did not well avis'd it vew,
 Would surely deeme it to be yvie trew:
 Low his lascivious armes adown did creepe,
 That sometimes dipping in the silver dew,
 Their fleecy flowres they tenderly did steepe,
Which drops of Christall seem'd for wantones to weepe.

Infinit streames, continually did well
 Out of the fountaine, sweet and faire to see,

The which into an ample laver fell,
And shortly grew to so great quantitie,
That like a little lake it seem'd to bee;
Whose depth exceeded not three cubits hight,
That through the waves one might the bottom see,
All pav'd beneath with jaspar shining bright,
That seem'd the fountaine in that see did sayle upright.

EDMUND SPENSER

WATER

Unlimited quantities of water from icy springs in the Appennines allowed a Renaissance Cardinal (and son of Lucretia Borgia) to create one of the world's most famous water gardens at the Villa d'Este at Tivoli, a hill town just east of Rome. He used it for fantastic fountains, cascades, falls, jets and water-fireworks of every kind. Siegfried Sassoon was a quintessential English author, but he has caught its magic.

Some of that magic can be introduced to even the most modest town gardens. Used subtly, water can enhance a garden by reflecting the changing moods of the sky or the form and colour of the surrounding vegetation. Images on its surface change as frequently as the patterns of foliage nudged by a breeze; disturbed by the air they can appear placid, turbulent, sombre, joyful or tumultuous all within minutes. Made to tumble down shady cascades, water will also markedly freshen the atmosphere.

Since it commands observation, a water surface can extend vistas by leading the eye deep into the garden, particularly if the water is confined to narrow streams or canals.

A water garden does not have to be vast to convey its delights but it must be more than the average small stone pool which has passed for water gardening in recent years. To be telling, water must be introduced to a garden with a sure eye and entire conviction.

Fortunately, recent technology enables us to indulge in water gardening on a grander scale. Reinforced, simulated-stone canal units are becoming available, light enough to be lifted into place by two men. They can be linked together directly or over weirs to form long runs. Even at thirty inches they are wide enough to be effective, but narrow enough to appear well in scale when laid out in small gardens. Their eight-inch depth gives root space for the majority of water plants and they can be filled and replenished with water economically so the demand for solid foundations is minimal.

Plants like water lilies, which need more water, can be grown in deeper pools (domestic water storage tanks are ideal) set separately or connected to the canal system by weirs.

Years of research into water movement has led to the production of special units which can be linked together to provide cascades which when fed with only relatively small amounts of water will maximize its turbulence to give beautiful effects while at the same time acting as a valuable and highly efficient oxygenator. These units can be arranged one below the other to create falls varying from a few inches to several feet in height. They make splendid entry or exit points for water in ponds or canals.

G.R.

*The Natural Garden
and the
Wild Garden*

A NATURAL WILDNESS

For the heath, which was the third part of our plot, I wish it to be framed, as much as may be, to a natural wildness. Trees I would have none in it; but some thickets, made only of sweet-briar and honeysuckle, and some wild vine amongst; and the ground set with violets, strawberries, and primroses. For these are sweet, and prosper in the shade. And these to be in the heath, here and there, not in any order. I like also little heaps, in the nature of mole-hills (such as are in wild heaths), to be set, some with wild thyme; some with pinks; some with germander, that gives a good flower to the eye; some with periwinkle; some with violets; some with strawberries; some with cowslips; some with daisies; some with red roses; some with lilium convallium; some with sweet-williams red; some with bear's-foot; and the like low flowers, being withal sweet and sightly. Part of which heaps to be with standards of little bushes pricked upon their top, and part without. The standards to be roses; juniper; holly; berberries (but here and there, because of the smell of their blossom); red currants; gooseberries; rosemary; sweet-briar; and such like. But these standards to be kept with cutting, that they grow not out of course.

For the side grounds, you are to fill them with variety of alleys, private, to give a full shade, some of them, wheresoever the sun be. You are to frame some of them likewise for shelter, that when the wind blows sharp, you may walk as in a gallery. And those alleys must be likewise hedged at both ends, to keep out the wind; and these closer alleys must be ever finely gravelled, and no grass, because of going wet. In many of these alleys likewise, you are to set fruit-trees of all sorts; as well upon the walls as in ranges. And this would be generally observed, that the borders, wherein you plant your fruit-trees, be fair and large, and low, and not steep; and set with fine flowers, but thin and sparingly, lest they deceive the trees. At the end of both the side grounds, I would have a mount of some pretty height, leaving the wall of the enclosure breast high, to look abroad into the fields.

For the main garden, I do not deny but there should be some fair alleys, ranged on both sides with fruit-trees; and some pretty tufts of fruit-trees, and arbours with seats, set in some decent order; but these to be by no means set too thick; but to leave the main garden so as it be not close, but the air open and free. For as for shade, I would have you rest upon the alleys of the side grounds, there to walk, if you be disposed, in the heat of the year or day; but to make account that the main garden is for the more temperate parts of the year; and in the heat of summer, for the morning and the evening, or over-cast days.

FRANCIS BACON

THE GENIUS OF THE PLACE

Something there is, more needful than Expence,
And something previous ev'n to Taste—'tis Sense:
Good Sense, which only is the gift of Heav'n,
And tho' no Science, fairly worth the seven:
A Light, which in yourself you must perceive;
Jones and le Nôtre have it not to give.

To build, to plant, whatever you intend,
To rear the Column, or the Arch to bend,
To swell the Terras, or to sink the Grot;

In all, let Nature never be forgot.
But treat the Goddess like a modest fair,
Nor over-dress, nor leave her wholly bare;
Let not each beauty ev'ry where be spy'd,
Where half the skill is decently to hide.
He gains all points, who pleasingly confounds,
Surprizes, varies, and conceals the Bounds.
   Consult the Genius of the Place in all;
That tells the Waters or to rise, or fall,
Or helps th'ambitious Hill the heav'ns to scale,
Or scoops in circling theatres the Vale;
Calls in the Country, catches op'ning glades,
Joins willing woods, and varies shades from shades;
Now breaks, or now directs, th'intending Lines,
Paints as you plant, and as you work, designs.
   Still follow Sense, of ev'ry Art the Soul,
Parts answ'ring parts shall slide into a whole,
Spontaneous beauties all around advance,
Start ev'n from Difficulty, strike from Chance;
Nature shall join you;

ALEXANDER POPE

ON KENT THE GARDENER

Painter enough to taste the charms of landscape, bold and opinionate enough to dare to dictate, and born with the genius to strike out a great system from the twilight of imperfect essays. He felt the delicious contrast of hill and valley changing imperceptibly into each other – remarked how loose groves crowned an easy eminence with happy ornament, and while they called in the distant view between their graceful stems, removed and extended the perspective of delusive comparison. But of all the beauties he added to this beautiful country none surpassed his management of water. Adieu to canals, circular basins, and cascades tumbling down marble steps, that last absurd magnificence of Italian and French villas. The gentle stream was taught to serpentine seemingly at its pleasure, and where discontinued by different levels its course appeared to be concealed by thickets properly interspersed, and glittered away at a distance where it might be supposed naturally to arrive.

HORACE WALPOLE

ON CHARLES BRIDGEMAN

He banished verdant sculpture and did not even revert to the square precision of the foregoing age. He disdained to make every division tally to its opposite, and though he still adhered to strait walks with high clipped hedges, they were only his great lines; the rest he diversified by wildernesses, and with loose groves of oak, though still within surrounding hedges. But the capital stroke ... was the destruction of walls for boundaries, and the invention of fosses – an attempt then deemed so astonishing, that the common people called them Ha! Ha's! to express their surprize at finding a sudden and unperceived check to their walk. – The contiguous ground of the park without the sunk fence was to be harmonised with the lawn within; and the garden in its turn was to be set free from its prim regularity, that it might assort with the wilder country without.

HORACE WALPOLE

THAT PRIMITIVE STATE

I shall no longer resist the passion growing in me for things of a natural kind, where neither art nor the caprice of man has spoilt the genuine order by breaking in upon that primitive state. Even the rude rocks, the mossy caverns, the irregular unwrought grottoes and broken falls of water, with all the horrid graces of the wilderness itself, in representing nature more, will be the more engaging, and appear with a magnificence beyond the mockery of princely gardens.

ASHLEY COOPER

NATURE EXALTED BY ART

Nature which we find in the English gardens is no longer the same nature as the one we had left outside. It is a nature enlivened by a soul, a nature exalted by art, which delights not only the simple man, but the man of education and culture; the one she teaches to think, the other to feel.

SCHILLER

THE YORKSHIRE GARDEN

Happy art thou if thou canst call thine own
Such scenes as these: where Nature and where
    Time
Have worked congenial, where a scatter'd host
Of antique oaks darken thy sidelong hills;
While, rushing thro' their branches, rifted cliffs
Dart their white heads, and glitter thro' the gloom.

REV. WILLIAM MASON

THE CHARM OF NATURE

Dame Nature is a gentle woman. No guide's fee will obtain her favour, no abrupt demand; hardly will she bear questioning, or direct curious gazing at her beauty; least of all will she reveal it truly to the hurried glance of a passing traveller, while he waits for his dinner or fresh horses, or fuel or water; always we must quietly and unimpatiently wait upon her. Gradually and silently the charm comes over us, the beauty has entered our souls. We know not exactly when nor how, but going away we remember it with a tender, subdued, filial-like joy.

Does this seem nonsense to you? Very likely, for I am talking of what I don't understand. Nature treats me so strangely; it is past my speaking sensibly of it, and yet, as part of my travelling experience, I should speak of it. At times I seem myself to be her favourite, and she brings me to my knees in deep feeling, such as she blesses no other with; oftener I see others in ecstacies, while I am left to sentimentalise and mourn, or to be critical and sneering, and infidel. Nonsense still – but tell me, do you think it is only for greed of trout that your great sensitive man lingers long, intently stooping over dark pools in the spray of the mountain torrents, or stealing softly away through the bended rushes, or kneeling lowly on the darkest verdure of the wooded meadow. What else? I know not what he thinks, but of this I am assured – while his mind is not intent upon his trivial sport his heart and soul will be far more absorbed of the rugged strength, the diffuse impetuous brilliance and the indefinite gliding grace or the beautiful twilight loveliness of the scene around him, than if he went out searching, labouring directly for it as for bread or fame.

FREDERICK OLMSTEAD

A FRENCH PARK, WILD AND UNDECORATED

It consists of three distinct water scenes; or of two lakes and a river. We were first shown that which is so famous for the small isle of poplars, in which reposes all that was mortal of that extraordinary and inimitable writer [Jean Jacques Rousseau]. This scene is as well imagined, and as well executed as could be wished. The water is between forty and fifty acres; hills rise from it on both sides, and it is sufficiently closed in by tall wood at both ends, to render it sequestered. The remains of departed genius stamp a melancholy idea, from which decoration would depart too much, and accordingly there is little.

We viewed the scene in a still evening. The declining sun threw a lengthened shade on the lake, and silence seemed to repose on its unruffled bosom; as some poet says, I forget who. The worthies to whom the temple of philosophies is dedicated, and whose names are marked on the columns, are NEWTON, *Lucem.*— DESCARTES, *Nil in rebus inane*—VOLTAIRE, *Ridiculum*—ROUSSEAU, *Naturam*—And on another unfinished column, *Quis hoc perficiet?*

The other lake is larger; it nearly fills the bottom of the vale, around which are some rough, rocky, wild and barren sand hills; either broken or spread with heath; in some places wooded, and in others scattered thinly with junipers. The character of the scene is that of wild and undecorated nature, in which the hand of art was meant to be concealed as much as was consistent with ease of access.

ARTHUR YOUNG

A HUMORIST IN GARDENING

I am one, you must know, who is looked upon as a humorist in gardening. I have several acres about my house, which I call my garden, and which a skilful gardener would not know what to call. It is a confusion of kitchen and parterre, orchard and flower-garden, which lie so mixt and interwoven with one another, that if a foreigner, who had seen nothing of our country, should be conveyed into my garden at his first landing, he would look upon it as a natural wilderness, and one of the uncultivated parts of our country. My flowers grow up in several parts of the garden in the greatest luxuriancy and profusion. I am so far from being fond of any particular one, by reason of its rarity, that if I meet with any one in a field which pleases me, I give it a place in my garden. By this means, when a stranger walks with me, he is surprised to see large spots of ground covered with ten thousand different colours, and has often singled out flowers he might have met with under a common hedge, in a field, or in a meadow, as some of the greatest beauties of the place. The only method I observe in this particular, is to range in the same quarter the products of the same season, that they may make their appearance together, and compose a picture of the greatest variety. There is the same irregularity in my plantations, which run into as great a wilderness as their natures will permit. I take in none that do not naturally rejoice in the soil; and am pleased, when I am walking, in a labyrinth of my own raising, not to know whether the next tree I shall meet with is an apple or an oak; an elm or a pear tree.

JOSEPH ADDISON

BY NO MEANS IMITATE NATURE

Large or small, the garden should look both orderly and rich. It should be well fenced from the outer world. It should by no means imitate either the wilfulness or the wildness of Nature, but should look like a thing never seen except near a house.

WILLIAM MORRIS

TINTERN ABBEY

June 30, 1875

I climbed to the top of the walls and looked down into the vast square deep well formed by the four great lofty arches of nave, choir and transepts which upheld the great central tower of the Church. The top of the walls was adorned with a perfect wild-flower garden of scarlet poppies, white roses, yellow stonecrop and purple mallows, which formed a low hedge along each side of the otherwise undefended footpath or thickness of the walls, and which climbed with profuse luxuriance over the ruins of the summit of the walls. From this perch, on a level with jackdaws ... I looked down into the green-floored enclosure of the grey ruins and into the streets of the village where the people looked dreadfully small as they moved about the roads and garden paths.

REV. FRANCIS KILVERT

FOR THE ORGANIC GARDEN

Of composts shall the Muse descend to sing,
Nor soil her heavenly plumes? The sacred Muse

Naught sordid deems, but what is base; naught fair
Unless true Virtue stamp it with her seal.
Then, planter, wouldst thou double thine estate,
Never, ah never, be ashamed to tread
Thy dung-heaps, where the refuse of thy mills,
With all the ashes, all thy coppers yield,
With weeds, mould, dung and stale, a compost form,
Of force to fertilize the poorest soil . . .
　　Whether the fattening compost in each hole
'Tis best to throw, or on the surface spread,
Is undetermined: trials must decide.
Unless kind rains and fostering dews descend,
To melt the compost's fertilizing salts,
A stinted plant, deceitful of thy hopes,
Will from those beds slow spring where hot dung lies:
But, if 'tis scattered generously o'er all,
The cane will better bear the solar blaze;
Less rain demand; and, by repeated crops,
Thy land improved its gratitude will show.
　　Enough of composts, Muse . . .

JAMES GRAINGER

NATURE PREFERRED

"In England," said Poirot, "people show you their
herbaceous borders and they take you to see their roses
and they talk at inordinate length about their iris
gardens, and to show they appreciate one of the great
beauties of England, they take you on a day when the
sun shines and the beech trees are in leaf, and
underneath them are all the bluebells. Yes, it is a very
beautiful sight, but I have been shown it, I think, once
too often. I prefer—" the thought broke off in his mind
as he thought back to what he had preferred. A drive

through Devon lanes. A winding road with great banks
going up each side of it, and on those banks a great
carpet and showing of primroses. So pale, so subtly and
timidly yellow, and coming from them that sweet, faint,
elusive smell that the primrose has in large quantities,
which is the smell of spring almost more than any other
smell. And so it would not be all rare shrubs here.
There would be spring and autumn, there would be
little wild cyclamen and there would be autumn crocus
here too. It was a beautiful place.

AGATHA CHRISTIE

ALLOTMENTS IN NATURE

From the vale where the Branscombe pours its clear
waters through rough masses of shingle into the sea the
ground to the east rises steeply to a height of nearly five
hundred feet; the cliff is thus not nearly so high as many
another, but it has features of peculiar interest. Here, in
some former time, there has been a landslip, a large
portion of the cliff at its highest part falling below and
forming a sloping mass of chalky soil mingled with huge
fragments of rock, which lies like a buttress against the
vertical precipice and seems to lend it support . . . On
this rough slope, under the shelter of the cliff, with the
sea at its feet, the villagers have formed their cultivated
patches. The patches, wildly irregular in form, some on
such steeply sloping ground as to suggest the idea that
they must have been cultivated on all fours, are divided
from each other by ridges and by masses of rock, deep
fissures in the earth, strips of bramble and thorn and
furze bushes. Altogether the effect was very singular;
the huge rough mass of jumbled rock and soil, the ruin

wrought by Nature in one of her Cromwellian moods, and, scattered irregularly about its surface, the plots or patches of cultivated smoothness – potato rows, green parallel lines ruled on a grey ground, and big, blue-green, equidistant cabbage-globes – each plot with its fringe of spike-like onion leaves, crinkled parsley, and other garden herbs. Here the villagers came by a narrow, steep, and difficult path they had made, to dig in their plots; while overhead, the gulls, careless of their presence, pass and repass wholly occupied with their own affairs.

W.H. HUDSON

NATURAL GARDEN

Gardeners must tolerate a degree of disorder if they wish to participate in conservation by creating useful habitats for wildlife. Although the garden may be cultivated fairly conventionally close in to the house, much of it must be left as wilderness where nature can run wild. But nothing must be too orderly – no beds packed with annuals – rather traditional plants whose flowers seem to offer better-quality nectar than those of new hybrids.

The lawn should be mown but not manicured, hedges can be thick but they mustn't be clipped and the bases of trees and shrubs should be allowed to frill enthusiastically. Honesty should be left to seed everywhere to provide nectar for orange tip butterflies. Their caterpillars thrive on the leaves of cuckoo pint which likes moist hedge bottoms. Ice plants, lavender, perennial sweet pea, buddleia, honeysuckle, Albertine roses and antirrhinums also make excellent insect fodder.

On stream or pond edges skyscraper bullrushes can provide cosy nesting for ducks, moorhens and coots. The parasols of giant hogweed induce aerobatic fantasies in goldfinches, bull-finches and siskins as they snatch its nutritious seed. Harvest mice convert tall reeds into high-rise apartments while in the secluded sanctuary of their undergrowth bitterns find perfect parking.

Large and small white butterflies, peacocks and wall butterflies can convert thick drifts of pale mauve great hairy willow herb in a wilderness area into a kaleidoscope of colour in summer. And later when the seed is ripe it makes a great pull-up for birds.

Using more erect plants as a natural trellis, field bindweed can cover the ground with a green mattress which fairly throbs with life. Bees pillage its deep bell flowers for nectar while in the sauna-damp gloom beneath the leaves, frogs and toads luxuriate.

An old orchard left untended where the boughs are ivy-clad can become a wildlife motel sheltering a vibrant world of birds, insects and small mammals.

You don't have to do much to establish a wildlife garden. If you create the right conditions initially and then leave it well alone, nature will do the rest.

G.R.

Perspectives

JAPANESE ILLUSION

It is paved with blue pebbles, and its centre is occupied by a pondlet—a miniature lake fringed with rare plants, and containing a tiny island, with tiny mountains and dwarf peach-trees and pines and azaleas, some of which are perhaps more than a century old, though scarcely more than a foot high. Nevertheless, this work, seen as it was intended to be seen, does not appear to the eye in miniature at all. From a certain angle of the guest-room looking out upon it, the appearance is that of a real lake shore with a real island beyond it, a stone's throw away. So cunning the art of the ancient gardener who contrived all this, and who has been sleeping for a hundred years under the cedars of Gesshoji, that the illusion can be detected only from the *zashiki* by the presence of an *ishidōrō*, or stone lamp, upon the island. The size of the *ishidōrō* betrays the false perspective, and I do not think it was placed there when the garden was made.

LAFCADIO HEARN

HA-HA

A wooden arch is bent astride
A ditch of water, four feet wide,
With angles, curves and zig-zag lines
From Halfpenny's exact designs.
In front, a level lawn is seen,
Without a shrub upon the green,
Where taste would want its first great law
But for the skulking, sly ha-ha,
By whose miraculous assistance
You gain a prospect two fields distance.

ROBERT LLOYD

ART AND TASTE

Mr. Pope undoubtedly contributed to form Kent's taste. The design of the Prince of Wales's garden at Carlton House was evidently borrowed from the poet's at Twickenham. There was little affected modesty in the latter, when he said, of all his works he was most proud of his garden. And yet it was a singular effort of art and taste to impress so much variety and scenery on a spot of five acres. The passing through the gloom from the grotto to the opening day, the retiring and again assembling shades, the dusky groves, the larger lawn and the solemnity of the termination of the cypresses that led up to his mother's tomb, are managed with exquisite judgement; and though Lord Peterborough assisted him to form his quincunx and to rank his vines, those were not the most pleasing ingredients of his little perspective.

HORACE WALPOLE

MORE TASTE

Sterling: How d'ye like these close walks, my Lord?
Lord Ogleby: A most excellent serpentine! It forms a perfect maze, and winds like a true lover's knot.
Sterling: Ay, here's none of your straight lines here—but all taste—zigzag—crinkum-crankum—in and out—right and left—to and again—twisting and turning like a worm, my Lord.

DAVID GARRICK AND GEORGE COLMAN

IT SHOULD GIVE THE APPEARANCE OF EXTENT

"It wants improvement, ma'am, beyond anything. I never saw a place that wanted so much improvement in my life ... I hope I shall have some good friend to help me."

"Your best friend upon such an occasion," said Miss Bertram calmly, "could be Mr Repton, I imagine ... His terms are five guineas a day."

JANE AUSTEN

The perfection of landscape gardening consists in the four following requisites: *First* it must display the natural beauties, and hide the natural defects of every situation. *Secondly* it should give the appearance of extent and freedom, by carefully disguising or hiding the boundary. *Thirdly* it must studiously conceal every inference of art, however expensive, by which the natural scenery is improved ... *Fourthly* all objects of mere convenience or comfort, if incapable of being made ornamental ... must be removed or concealed.

HUMPHREY REPTON

PERSPECTIVES

The work of Humphrey Repton (1752–1818), one of the most influential of British landscape gardeners, can still be seen, virtually untouched, at Rousham near Oxford. Jane Austen was more a chronicler of the drama of the drawing room than of the garden, but she showed a sure touch when IMPROVEMENTS were needed because she knew that Repton's were essentially illusionary. Note how clear his Requisite No. 2 is on the point.

Optical illusions applied to the making of a garden are very much in the tradition of the landscapers like Repton who 'extended' views by the adroit manipulation of sight lines. They reinforced the effect by using graduated colours in planting schemes to create an illusion of depth. They, of course, conducted their optical tricks at some scale, pandering to wealthy patrons and their notions of grandeur. Yet, although the principles they used in constructing enticing perspectives have long been understood, little use has been made of them, scaled down, in the smaller garden. This is a great pity.

Limitation of size is the commonest problem which modern garden designers have to overcome. The typical town plot offers little sense of vista. Everything is seen to be exactly what and where it is – slap against the window with the far boundary only a coin's flick away, all enclosed and contained, with no element of mystery.

The idea of using optical trickery in the small garden is not as preposterous as it sounds, for the eye makes fairly rigid assumptions and can easily be deceived. Feed it a path whose sides gradually taper and it sees parallel sides stretching into a further distance – a trick you can play just as effectively with false horizontals in pergolas and trellises.

A truly geometrical interpretation of perspective is impossible in a practical garden. For example, timber used to make a 'perspective' trellis will have to diminish so much in its dimensions as to lose its mechanical strength. Another example is the arch; if it is to be low enough to lower the perspective, you will not be able to walk under it.

So the designer must make compromises, establishing different vanishing points for different features such as paths and trellises. A garden could appear to consist of a number of circles – or what appear to be circles – but in fact as they go into the distance they become progressively flattened elipses. It is all a matter for the designer's eye – tapering walls and trellises, making support posts of decreasing size and setting them more closely together.

Pope wrote: 'He gains all points who pleasingly confounds, surprises, varies and conceals the bounds,' so use visual tricks with discretion; bold architectural planting with bright-leaved coloured subjects near the house and fine-leaved foliage in much paler shades at the far end to help exaggerate the length of the garden; or rustic arches of diminishing width. False arches in the side walls give an illusion of breadth – and a tapering and winding path adds to the sense of mystery and appears to give length to the vista.

G.R.

E. du Plessis Ho...

Cottage Gardens,
Kitchen Gardens
and Orchards

THOSE OLD-FASHIONED PARADIES

The garden was one of those old-fashioned paradies which hardly exist any longer except as memories of our childhood. No finical separation between flower and kitchen garden there, no monotony of enjoyment for one sense to the exclusion of another, but a charming paradisiacal mingling of all that was pleasant to the eyes and good for food. The rich flower border running along every walk, with its endless succession of spring flowers, anemones, auriculas, wall-flowers, sweet williams, campanulas, snap dragons, and tiger lilies, had its tall beauties, such as moss and Provence roses, varied with espalier apple-trees; the crimson of a carnation was carried out in the lurking of the neighbouring strawberry beds.

GEORGE ELIOT

THE COTTAGE GARDEN

Want of general effect! Is there none in those cottage gardens, where the Nasturtiums twine lovingly all the summer amongst Jasmine, Clematis, and thickly trellised Rose—where the towering splendour of the Hollyhocks is confronted by the broad discs of the Sunflower, and where the huge leaves, herbs, and fruit-trees of the kitchen garden run close up on or intermix with the border flowers, amongst which we may meet at any time with some new or long-absent friend? Here are no masses of colour in the modern sense; but do you ever feel the want of them? Or can you turn from these simple plots, unstudied for effect, to the showy, unvaried brilliancy of the modern border, and find that you miss nothing there? Do not the plants seem comparatively wanting in interest? Do they not seem to be individually less dear, to hold you with a lighter grasp?

FORBES WATSON

WHO CAN ENDURE A CABBAGE BED IN OCTOBER?

—"It was always a very comfortable House—said Mrs Parker—looking at it through the back window with something like the fondness of regret.—And such a nice garden—such an excellent Garden." "Yes, my Love, but *that* we may be said to carry with us.—It supplies us, as before, with all the fruit & vegetables we want; & we have in fact all the comfort of an excellent Kitchen Garden, without the constant Eyesore of its formalities; or the yearly nuisance of its decaying vegetation.—Who can endure a Cabbage Bed in October?" "Oh! dear—yes.—We are quite as well off for Gardenstuff as ever we were—for if it is forgot to be brought at any time, we can always buy what we want at Sanditon House.—The Gardiner there, is glad enough to supply us—.

JANE AUSTEN

AFTER READING IN A LETTER PROPOSALS FOR BUILDING A COTTAGE

A little garden, not too fine,
Enclose with painted pales;
And woodbines, round the cot to twine,

Pin to the wall with nails.

Let hazels grow, and spindling sedge,
Bend bowering overhead;
Dig old man's beard from woodland hedge,
To twine a summer shade.

Beside the threshold sods provide,
And build a summer seat;
Plant sweet-briar bushes by its side,
And flowers that blossom sweet.

JOHN CLARE

CARE IS THE LADIES' PART

In every garden, four things are necessary to be
provided for—flowers, fruit, shade, and water; and
whoever lays out a garden without all these, must not
pretend it in any perfection. It ought to lie to the best
parts of the house, or to those of the master's
commonest use; so as to be but like one of the rooms
out of which you step into another. The part of your
garden next your house (besides the walks that go round
it), should be a parterre for flowers, or grass plots,
bordered with flowers; or if, according to the newest
mode, it be cast all into grass plots and gravel walks, the
dryness of these should be relieved with fountains, and
the plainness of those with statues; otherwise, if large,
they have an ill effect upon the eye. However, the part
next the house should be open, and no other fruit upon
the walls. If this take up one half of the garden, the other
should be fruit-trees, unless some grove for shade lie in
the middle; if it take up a third part only, then the next

third may be dwarf trees, and the last standard fruit; or else the second part fruit-trees, and the third all sorts of winter-greens, which provide for all seasons of the year. I will not enter upon any account of flowers, having only pleased myself with seeing or smelling them, and not troubled myself with the care, which is more the ladies' part than the men's; but the success is wholly in the gardener.

SIR WILLIAM TEMPLE

MR. ROCHESTER'S CIGAR

I walked a while on the pavement; but a subtle, well-known scent—that of a cigar—stole from some window; I saw the library casement open a hand-breadth; I knew I might be watched thence; so I went apart into the orchard. No nook in the grounds more sheltered and more Eden-like; it was full of trees, it bloomed with flowers: a very high wall shut it out from the court, on one side; on the other, a beech avenue screened it from the lawn. At the bottom was a sunk fence; its sole separation from lonely fields: a winding walk, bordered with laurels and terminating in a giant horse-chestnut, circled at the base by a seat, led down to the fence. Here one could wander unseen. While such honey-dew fell, such silence reigned, such gloaming gathered, I felt as if I could haunt such shade for ever: but in threading the flower and fruit-parterres at the upper part of the inclosure, enticed there by the light the now-risen moon casts on this more open quarter, my step is stayed—not by sound, not by sight, by once more by a warning fragrance.

Sweet briar and southernwood, jasmine, pink, and

rose, have long been yielding their evening sacrifice of incense: this new scent is neither of shrub nor flower; it is—I know it well—it is Mr. Rochester's cigar. I look around and I listen. I see trees laden with ripening fruit. I hear a nightingale warbling in a wood half a mile off; no moving form is visible, no coming step audible; but that perfume increases: I must flee. I make for the wicket leading to the shrubbery, and I see Mr. Rochester entering. I step aside into the ivy recess, he will not stay long: he will soon return whence he came, and if I sit still he will never see me.

But no—eventide is as pleasant to him as to me, and this antique garden as attractive; and he strolls on, now lifting the gooseberry-tree branches to look at the fruit, large as plums, with which they are laden; now taking a ripe cherry from the wall; now stooping towards a knot of flowers, either to inhale their fragrance or to admire the dew-beads on their petals. A great moth goes humming by me: it alights on a plant at Mr. Rochester's foot: he sees it, and bends to examine it.

"Now, he has his back towards me," thought I, "and he is occupied too; perhaps, if I walk softly, I can slip away unnoticed."

I trod on an edging of turf that the crackle of the pebbly gravel might not betray me: he was standing among the beds at a yard or two distant from where I had to pass; the moth apparently engaged him. "I shall get by very well," I meditated. As I crossed his shadow, thrown long over the garden by the moon, not yet risen high, he said quietly without turning:—

"Jane, come and look at this fellow."

CHARLOTTE BRONTË

OUR VILLAGE, OUR GARDEN

The pride of my heart and the delight of my eyes is my garden. Our house, which is in dimensions very like a bird-cage, and might, with almost equal convenience, be laid on a shelf or hung up in a tree, would be utterly unbearable in wet weather were it not that we have a retreat out of doors, and a very pleasant retreat it is. To make my readers comprehend it I must describe our whole territories.

Fancy a small plot of ground with a pretty, low, irregular cottage at one end; a large granary, divided from the dwelling by a little court running along one side; and a long thatched shed, open towards the garden, and supported by wooden pillars, on the other. The bottom is bounded half by an old wall and half by an old paling, over which we see a pretty distance of woody hills. The house, granary, wall, and paling, are covered with vines, cherry-trees, roses, honeysuckles, and jessamines, with great clusters of tall hollyhocks running up between them; a large elder overhanging the little gate, and a magnificent bay-tree, such a tree as shall scarcely be matched in these parts, breaking with its beautiful conical form the horizontal lines of the buildings. This is my garden; and the long pillared shed, the sort of rustic arcade, which runs along one side, parted from the flower-beds by a row of geraniums, is our out-of-door drawing-room.

I know nothing so pleasant as to sit there on a summer afternoon, with the western sun flickering through the great elder-tree, and lighting up our gay parterres, where flowers and flowering shrubs are set as thick as grass in a field, a wilderness of blossom, interwoven, intertwined, wreathy, garlandy, profuse beyond all profusion, where we may guess that there is such a thing as mould, but never see it. I know nothing so pleasant as to sit in the shade of that dark bower, with the eye resting on that bright piece of colour, lighted so gloriously by the evening sun, now catching a glimpse of the little birds as they fly rapidly in and out of their nests—for there are always two or three birds'-nests in the thick tapestry of cherry-trees, honeysuckles, and china-roses, which cover our walls—now tracing the gay gambols of the common butterflies as they sport around the dahlias; now watching that rarer moth, which the country people, fertile in pretty names, call the bee-bird; that bird-like insect, which flutters in the hottest days over the sweetest flowers, inserting its long proboscis into the small tube of the jessamine, and hovering over the scarlet blossom of the geranium, whose bright colour seems reflected on its own feathery breast: that insect which seems so thoroughly a creature of the air, never at rest; always, even when feeding, self-poised and self-supported, and whose wings, in their ceaseless motion, have a sound so deep, so full, so lulling, so musical. Nothing so pleasant as to sit amid that mixture of rich flowers and leaves, watching the bee-bird! Nothing so pretty to look at as my garden! It is quite a picture; only unluckily it resembles a picture in more qualities than one—it is fit for nothing but to look at. One might as well think of walking in a bit of framed canvas. There are walks, to be sure—tiny paths of smooth gravel, by courtesy called such—but they are so overhung by roses and lilies, and such gay encroachers—so overrun by convolvulus, and heart's-ease, and mignonette, and other sweet stragglers, that, except to edge through them occasionally for the purpose of planting, or weeding, or watering, there might as well be no paths at all. Nobody thinks of walking in my garden. Even May glides along with a delicate and trackless step, like a swan through the water; and we, its two-footed denizens, are fain to treat it as if it were really a saloon, and go out for a walk towards sunset, just as if we had not been sitting in the open air all day.

MARY RUSSELL MITFORD

EVERYTHING USEFUL FOR THE KITCHEN

No parterres, no fountains, no statues, embellished this little garden. Its only ornament was a short walk, shaded on each side by a filbert-hedge, with a small alcove at one end, whither in hot weather the gentleman and his wife used to retire and divert themselves with their children, who played in the walk before them. But, though vanity had no votary in this little spot, here was a variety of fruit and everything useful for the kitchen, which was abundantly sufficient to catch the admiration of Adams, who told the gentleman he had certainly a good gardener. Sir, answered he, that gardener is now before you; whatever you see here is the work solely of my own hands. Whilst I am providing necessaries for my table, I likewise procure myself an appetite for them.

HENRY FIELDING

CYDER

The *Pippin* burnish'd o'er with Gold, the *Moile*
Of sweetest hony'd Taste, the fair *Permain*,
Temper'd, like comliest Nymph, with red and white.

Salopian Acres flourish with a Growth
Peculiar, styl'd the *Ottley*: Be thou first
This Apple to transplant; if to the Name
Its Merit answers, no where shalt thou find
A Wine more priz'd, or laudable of Taste.
Nor does the *Eliot* least deserve thy Care,
Nor *John-Apple*, whose wither'd Rind, entrencht
With many a Furrow, aptly represents
Decrepid Age: nor that from *Harvey* nam'd
Quick-relishing: Why should we sing the *Thrift*,
Codling, or *Pomroy*, or of pimpled Coat
The *Russet*, or the *Cat's Head's* weighty Orb
Enormous in its Growth: for various Use
Tho' these are meet, tho' after full repast
Are oft requir'd, and crown the rich Desert?
    What, tho' the *Pear-Tree* rival not the Worth
Of Ariconian Products? Yet her Freight
Is not contemn'd, yet her wide-branching Arms
Best screen thy Mansion from the fervent Dog
Adverse to Life; the wintry Hurricanes
In vain imploy their Roar, her Trunc unmov'd
Breaks the strong Onset, and controls their Rage.
Chiefly the *Bosbury*, whose large Increase,
Annual, in sumptuous Banquets claims Applause.
Thrice acceptable Bev'rage! could but Art
Subdue the floating Lee, *Pomona's* self
Would dread thy Praise, and shun the dubious Strife.
Be it thy choice, when Summer-Heats annoy,
To sit beneath her leafy Canopy,
Quaffing rich Liquids: Oh! how sweet t' enjoy
At once her Fruits, and hospitable Shade!
    But how with equal number shall we match
The *Musk's* surpassing Worth! that earliest gives
Sure hopes of racy Wine, and in its Youth

Its tender Nonage, loads the spreading Boughs
With large and juicy Off-spring, that defies
The Vernal Nippings, and cold Syderal Blasts!
Yet let her to the *Red-Streak* yield, that once
Was of the Sylvan Kind, unciviliz'd,
Of no Regard, 'till Scudamore's skilful Hand
Improv'd her, and by courtly Discipline
Taught her the savage Nature to forget:
Hence styl'd the *Scudamorean* Plant; whose Wine
Who-ever tastes, let him with grateful Heart
Respect that ancient loyal House, and wish
The noble Peer, that now transcends our Hopes
In early Worth, his Country's justest Pride,
Uninterrupted Joy, and Health entire.

JOHN PHILIPS

ARCADIA

Some of these cottages in summer-time really approach
something of that Arcadian beauty which is supposed to
prevail in the country. Everything, of course, depends
upon the character of the inmates. The dull tint of the
thatch is relieved here and there by great patches of
sillgreen which is religiously preserved as a good herb,
though the exact ailments for which it is 'good' are often
forgotten. One end of the cottage is often completely
hidden with ivy, and woodbine grows in thickest
profusion over the porch. Near the door there are
almost always a few cabbage-rose trees, and under the
windows grow wall-flowers and hollyhocks, sweet peas,
columbine and sometimes the graceful lilies of the
valley. The garden stretches in a long strip from the
door, one mass of green. It is enclosed by thick hedges,

over which the dog-rose grows, and the wild convolvulus will blossom in the autumn. Trees fill up every available space and corner—apple trees, pear trees, damsons, plums, bullaces—all varieties. The cottages seem to like to have at least one tree of every sort. These trees look very nice in the spring when the apple blossom is out, and again in the autumn when the fruit is ripe. Under the trees are gooseberry bushes, raspberries and numbers of currants. The patches are divided into strips producing potatoes, cabbage, lettuce, onions, radishes, parsnips; in this kitchen produce, as with the fruit, they like to possess a few of all kinds. There is generally a great bunch of rhubarb. In odd corners there are sure to be a few specimens of southernwood, mugwort, and other herbs; not for use, but from adherence to the old customs. The old people thought much of these 'yjerbs', so they must have some too, as well as a little mint and similar potherbs. In the windows you may see two or three geraniums, and over the porch a wicker cage, in which the 'ousel cock, with orange-tawny bill', pours out his rich, melodious notes. There is hardly a cottage without its captive bird, or tame rabbit, or mongrel cur, which seems as much attached to his master as more high-bred dogs to their owners.

RICHARD JEFFERIES

DIM PREDICTIONS

It was only a short distance from the factory, but the hedge and high bank on each side of the lane which conducted to it seemed to give it something of the appearance and feeling of seclusion. It was a small

white-washed place, with a green porch over the door;
scanty brown stalks showed in the garden soil near this
porch, and likewise beneath the windows, stalks budless
and flowerless now, but giving dim prediction of trained
and blooming creepers for summer days. A grass plat
and borders fronted the cottage; the borders presented
only black mould yet, except where, in sheltered nooks,
the first shoots of snowdrop or crocus peeped, green as
emerald from the earth. The spring was late; it had been
a severe and prolonged winter; the last deep snow had
but just disappeared before yesterday's rains; on the
hills, indeed, white remnants of it yet gleamed, flecking
the hollows, and crowning the peaks; the lawn was not
verdant, but bleached, as was the grass on the bank and
under the hedge in the lane.

CHARLOTTE BRONTË

A REGULAR GARDEN

The cottage and its garden were so regular in their plan
that they might have been laid out by a Dutch designer
of the time of William and Mary. In a low, dense hedge
was a door, over which the hedge formed an arch, and
from the inside of the door a straight path, bordered
with clipped box, ran up the slope of the garden to the
porch, which was exactly in the middle of the house-
front, with two windows on each side. Right and left of
the path were first a bed of gooseberry bushes; next of
currant; next of raspberry; next of strawberry; next of
old fashioned flowers; at the corners opposite the porch
being spheres of box resembling a pair of school globes.

Over the roof of the house could be seen the

orchard on yet higher ground, and behind the orchard
the forest-trees, reaching to the crest of the hill.

THOMAS HARDY

A COMPLETE GARDEN

I got into the habit of creeping over to John's house, and
sitting for hours under the apple-trees in his garden. It
was now different from the wilderness he found it; the
old trees were pruned and tended, and young ones
planted. Mrs. Halifax called it proudly 'our orchard'
though the top of the tallest sapling could be reached
with her hand. Then, in addition to the indigenous
cabbages, came long rows of white-blossomed peas,
big-headed cauliflowers, and all vegetables easy of
cultivation. My father sent contributions from his
celebrated gooseberry-bushes, and his wall-fruit, the
pride of Norton Bury; Mrs. Jessop stocked the borders
from her great parterres of sweet-scented common
flowers; so that, walled in as it was, and in the midst of a
town likewise, it was growing into a very tolerable
garden. Just the kind of garden that I love – half-trim,
half-wild – fruits, flowers, and vegetables living in
comfortable equality and fraternity, none being too
choice to be harmed by their neighbours, none
esteemed too mean to be restricted in their natural
profusion. Oh, dear old-fashioned garden full of
sweet-williams and white-nancies, and larkspur and
London-pride, and yard-wide beds of snowy saxifrage,
and tall, pale evening primroses, and hollyhocks six or
seven feet high, many-tinted, from yellow to darkest
ruby-colour; while for scents, large blushing cabbage-
roses, pinks, gilly-flowers, with here and there a great

bush of southernwood or rosemary, or a border of thyme, or a sweet-briar hedge – a pleasant garden, where all colours and perfumes were blended together; ay, even a stray dandelion, that stood boldly up in his yellow waistcoat, like a young country bumpkin, who feels himself a decent lad in his way.

MRS CRAIK

GUIDE TO THE LAKES

These dwellings, mostly built, as has been said, of rough unknown stone, are roofed with slates, which were rudely taken from the quarry before the present art of splitting them was understood, and are, therefore, rough and uneven in their surface, so that both the covering and sides of the houses have furnished places of rest for the seeds of lichens, mosses, ferns and flowers. Hence buildings, which in their very form call to mind the processes of Nature, do thus, clothed in part with a vegetable garb, appear to be received into the bosom of the living principle of things, as it acts and exists among the woods and fields; and, by their colour and their shape, affect direct the thoughts to that tranquil course of Nature and simplicity, along which the humble-minded inhabitants have, through so many generations, been led. Add the little garden with its shed for bee-hives, its small bed of pot herbs, and its borders and patches of flowers for Sunday posies, with some-times a choice few too much prized to be plucked; an orchard of proportioned size; a cheese press, often supported by some tree near the door; a cluster of embowering sycamores for summer shade; with a tall fir, through which the winds sing when other trees are leafless; the little rill or household spout murmuring in all seasons; – combine these incidents and images together, and you have a representative idea of a mountain cottage in this country so beautifully formed in itself, and so richly adorned by the hand of Nature.

WILLIAM WORDSWORTH

A PLACE OF RETIREMENT

Low was our pretty Cot: our tallest rose
Peeped at the chamber-window. We could hear
At silent noon, and eve, and early morn,
The sea's faint murmur. In the open air
Our myrtles blossom'd; and across the porch
Thick jasmins twined: the little landscape
    round
Was green and woody, and refreshed the eye.
It was a spot which you might aptly call
The Valley of Seclusion!

SAMUEL TAYLOR COLERIDGE

A COTTAGE GARDEN

Where rustic taste at leisure trimly weaves
The rose and straggling woodbine to the eaves,
And on the crowded spot that pales enclose
The white and scarlet daisy rears in rows,
Training the trailing peas in clusters neat,
Perfuming evening with a luscious sweet –
And sunflowers planting for their gilded show,
That scale the window's lattice ere they blow,
And sweet to cottagers within the sheds,

Peep through the crystal panes their golden heads.

JOHN CLARE

A NATURAL WILDERNESS

My kitchen has likewise its particular quarters assigned to it; for besides the wholesome luxury which that place abounds with, I have always thought a kitchen-garden a more pleasant sight than the finest orangery, or artificial green-house. I love to see every thing in its perfection; and am more pleased to survey my rows of coleworts and cabbages, with a thousand nameless pot-herbs, springing up in their full fragrancy and verdure, than to see the tender plants of foreign countries kept alive by artificial heats, or withering in the air and soil that are not adapted to them. I must not omit, that there is a fountain rising in the upper part of my garden, which forms a little wandering rill, and administers to the pleasure as well as the plenty of the place. I have so conducted it, that it visits most of my plantations: and have taken particular care to let it run in the same manner as it would do in an open field, so that it generally passes through banks of violets and primroses, plats of willow, or other plants, that seem to be of its own producing. There is another circumstance in which I am very particular, or as my neighbours call me, very whimsical: as my garden invites into it all the birds of the country, by offering them the conveniency of springs and shades, solitude and shelter, I do not suffer any one to destroy their nests in the spring, or drive them from their usual haunts in fruit-time; I value my garden more for being full of blackbirds than cherries, and very frankly give them fruit for their songs. By this means, I have always the music of the season in its perfection, and am highly delighted to see the jay or the thrush hopping about my walks, and shooting before my eye across the several little glades and alleys that I pass through.

JOSEPH ADDISON

A TRUE FARMHOUSE GARDEN

Adam walked by the rick-yard, at present empty of ricks, to the little wooden gate leading into the garden—once the well-tended kitchen-garden of a manor-house; now, but for the handsome brick wall with stone coping that ran along one side of it, a true farmhouse garden, with hardy perennial flowers, un-pruned fruit-trees, and kitchen vegetables growing together in careless, half-neglected abundance. In that leafy, flowery, bushy time, to look for anyone in this garden was like playing at "hide-and-seek". There were the tall hollyhocks beginning to flower, and dazzle the eyes with their pink, white, and yellow; there were the syringas and Gueldres roses, all large and disorderly for want of trimming; there were leafy walls of scarlet beans and late peas; there was a row of bushy filberts in one direction, and in another a huge apple-tree making a barren circle under its low-spreading boughs. But what signified a barren patch or two? The garden was so large. There was always a superfluity of broad beans—it took nine or ten of Adam's strides to get to the end of the uncut grass walk that ran by the sides of them; and as for other vegetables, there was so much more room than was necessary for them, that in the rotation of crops a large flourishing bed of groundsel was of yearly occurrence on one spot or another. The very rose-trees, at which Adam stopped to pluck one, looked as if they grew wild; they were all huddled together in bushy masses, now flaunting with wide open petals, almost all of them of the streaked pink-and-white kind, which doubtless dated from the union of the houses of York and Lancaster. Adam was wise enough to choose a compact Provence rose that peeped out half-smothered by its flaunting scentless neighbours, and held it in his hand—he thought he should be more at ease holding something in his hand—as he walked on to the far end of the garden, where he remembered there was the largest row of currant-trees, not far off from the great yew-tree arbour.

GEORGE ELIOT

ONCE A LYNCHET

Our kitchen garden is separated from the cottage, and lies on the Knap some 50 yards away: half an acre of Dorset hillside rented for a nominal sum to keep us supplied with home-grown fruit and vegetables. Self-sufficiency was never our aim; but at least we are no longer totally dependent on the whims of fluctuating Euromarts. It's an odd piece of ground, like a double-decker slice of disused vineyard, drunkenly tilting as if about to lurch into the lane below. Once it was a lynchet, a medieval strip field. Perhaps it is of the same age as King Athelstan's castle on the other side of the valley. Certainly the Saxons had an eye for good land: our plot basks on a south-facing slope with a wall at its back, well drained and shielded from the prevailing south-westerlies by the flank of the hill. In the Middle

Ages flax might have grown there, blue as a summer sky, to be cropped, retted, scutched and hackled to provide yarn and sailcloth for West Country seamen.

Twenty years ago it had become a well-tended vegetable plot, diligently hoed, with onion beds and runner beans and a patch where free-range hens took dust baths in the sun. Eventually it proved too much for the old cottager who kept it, and the land fell fallow. In the space of a decade, nature took over. Where carrots and onions had fattened in orderly rows, brambles rolled in barbed wire tangles over infestations of nettles and rampant couch-grass. That was how it was when we arrived, like fugitives from the Monmouth Rebellion, armed with bramble scythes and long-handled slashers to reclaim the wilderness. When the brambles were vanquished and put to the torch there still remained the shock-headed clumps of couch to be cleared, sinewy hawsers of old man's beard, and nettle roots, gnarled and yellow, so stubbornly anchored in the earth that it took a mattock to prise them loose.

Now, looking back, it is hard to recognize that overgrown jungle in the wall-to-wall carpets of finely raked tilth, rich and deep like fine-ground coffee, and the burgeoning rows of sprouts and broccoli. Can this trim kitchen garden with its strawberry beds and fruit trees be the same unkempt battlefield where we burned the vengeful brambles and slew the nettlebeds ten years ago?

BRIAN JACKMAN

THE ORCHARD

The house itself was an ordinary white-washed, slate-roofed, French country house, with an immense walled fruit garden on the other side of it.

There was never such a garden, there never will be! Peaches, apricots, nectarines, and grapes of all kinds, lined the inside walls; the avenue that ran down the middle of it was of fig trees and standard peach trees. There were raspberries, cherries and strawberries, and flowers mingling with fruits and vegetables in a confusion the most charming in the world. Along the end of the garden was a great arcade of black, clipped yews, so thick and strong that a child could crawl on the outside of it without falling through.

E. NESBIT

COTTAGE GARDEN

As soon as farm workers began to drive big tractors during the week, and family saloons at the weekend, the allure of their traditional cottage gardens changed. Authentic cottage gardens were a wonderful higgledy-piggledy mixture of well-grown vegetable crops on knee-deep, fertile soil, fruit bushes for drying tea towels and 'smalls' as well as cropping, vast clumps of hardy perennials like irises, hollyhocks, lupins, and golden rod with an occasional knarled standard plum, apple or pear tree placed, it seemed, with no regard to any particular factor.

While the cottages themselves were mostly tumbledown this haphazard fecundity had great charm. Nowadays farm workers' wives understandably want the benefits of modern living. They seek the haven of the new council house with all its modern amenities. Brutalized by the constant buzz of the vast mechanical monsters which they drive, when they return in the evening their men share the town-dwellers' enjoyment of television. And at weekends, digging the garden has often less appeal than taking the family to the seaside.

The postcard, 'done-up', façades of the cottages in which farm workers used to live would sit uneasily behind a traditional cottage garden jumble. And real cottage gardens nowadays have been gentrified to match the new small-paned windows and sparkling paintwork. Sadly the effect is often absurd. Two schools of gardening seem to predominate – the chocolate-box extravaganza composed of literally thousands of garish annual plants, or the pseudo-grandiose, where an attempt has been made to convert a tiny rural patch into a version of Versailles. Neither approach is satisfactory.

Apart from trying to restore some of its former simplicity to the building, anyone acquiring such a property should think very hard about its garden. They should attempt to recapture some of its former beguiling charm. They may have been appropriate for Laurie Lee's mother, but vegetables can look very messy when serious cropping begins, so it is probably better to give them a less obvious home. Nowadays, using really intensive growing techniques, masses of produce can be gathered from a few 4ft x 4ft deep beds with plants grown more closely together.

Large irregularly shaped beds in which traditional herbaceous border plants are encouraged to establish large mounds and clumps can, if their colours are selected with restraint, replace the former vegetable plot with something more in character.

If they have been allowed to survive, some of the old fruit trees and soft fruit bushes or flowering shrubs should be allowed to develop their blousey natural form. Anything too tutored will seem suburban and out of place. Nothing as chic as a hybrid camellia, azalea or rhododendron or some of the more exotic shrubs being pushed at the garden centres should be planted in a good cottage garden. Old varieties of shrub rose, flowering currant, jasmine, syringa, lavender and buddleia are the types of shrub which look best.

G.R.

169

Parks and
Estates

OF THE PARKE OF THE GREAT CHAN KUBLAY

... The Citie Xandu, which the great Chan Kublay now raigning, built; erecting therein a marvellous and artificiall Palace of Marble and other stones, which abutteth on the wall to one side, and the midst of the Citie on the other. He included sixteen miles within the circuit of the wall on that side where the Palace abutteth on the Citie wall, into which none can enter but by the Palace. In this inclosure or Parke are goodly meadowes, springs, rivers, red and fallow Deere, Fawnes carried thither for the Hawkes (of which there are there above two hundred Gerfalcons which he goeth once a weeke to see), and he often vseth one Leopard or more, sitting on Horses, which he setteth vpon the Stagges and Deere, and having taken the beast, giveth it to the Gerfalcons; and in beholding this spectacle he taketh wonderfull delight. In the middest in a faire wood hee hath built a royall House on pillars gilded and vernished, on every of which is a Dragon all gilt, which windeth his tayle about the pillar, with his head bearing vp the loft, as also with his wings displayed on both sides: the cover also is of Reeds gilt and varnished, so that the raine can doe it no injurie, the reeds being three handfuls thicke and ten yards long, split from knot to knot. The house itselfe also may be sundred, and taken down like a Tent and erected againe. For it is sustained, when it is set vp, with two hundred silken Cords. Great *Chan* vseth to dwell there three moneths in the yeare, to wit, in June, July, and August. On the eight and twentieth day of August, he departeth to make a solemne sacrifice.

MARCO POLO

KUBLA KHAN

In Xanadu did Kubla Khan
A stately pleasure-dome decree:
Where Alph, the sacred river, ran
Through caverns measureless to man
   Down to a sunless sea.
So twice five miles of fertile ground
With walls and towers were girdled round:
And there were gardens bright with sinuous rills,
Where blossomed many an incense-bearing tree;
And here were forests ancient as the hills,
Enfolding sunny spots of greenery.

But oh! that deep romantic chasm which slanted
Down the green hill athwart a cedarn cover!
A savage place, as holy and enchanted
As e'er beneath a waning moon was haunted
By woman wailing for her demon-lover!
And from that chasm, with ceaseless turmoil seething,
As if this earth in fast thick pants were breathing,
A mighty fountain momently was forced:
Amid whose swift half-intermitted burst
Huge fragments vaulted like rebounding hail,
Or chaffy grain beneath the thresher's flail:
And 'mid these dancing rocks at once and ever
It flung up momently the sacred river.

SAMUEL TAYLOR COLERIDGE

THE PARK

He came downstairs. . . and began to roam through the
park, into which he let himself loose at first, and then, in

narrowing circles, through the nearer grounds. He rambled an hour in breathless ecstasy, brushing the dew from the deep fern and bracken and the rich borders of the garden, tasting the fragrant air and stopping everywhere, in murmuring rapture ... he had been dreaming all his life of just such a chance. It was the last of April, and everything was fresh and vivid; the great trees, in the early air, were a blur of tender shoots.

HENRY JAMES

A GARDEN AS BIG AS THE RITZ

The whole valley, from the diamond mountain to the steep granite cliff ... gave off a breath of golden haze which hovered idly above the fine sweep of lawns and lakes and gardens. Here and there, clusters of elms made delicate groves of shade, contrasting strangely with the tough masses of pine forest that held the hills in a grip of dark-blue green ... [The owner] had caused to be kidnapped a landscape gardener, an architect ... and a French decadent poet left over from the last century. He had put his entire force of negroes at their disposal, guaranteed to supply them with any materials that the world could offer.

F. SCOTT FITZGERALD

THROUGH ENGLAND ON A SIDE SADDLE

At Burghley, the house stands in a very fine park which is full of deer and fine rows of trees. On either side a very broad Glide or vista that looks finely to ye River and to the adjacent hills, a distance, both with fine woods.

CELIA FIENNES

ON AN ENGLISH PARK

I cannot undertake to describe the effects of so much taste and skill as have evidently been employed. I can only tell you that we passed by winding paths over acres and acres of a constant varying surface, where on all sides were growing every variety of shrubs and flowers, in more than natural growth, all set in borders of the closest turf; all kept with the most consummate neatness. At a distance of a quarter of a mile from the gate we came to an open field of clean bright green sward, closely mown, on which a large tent was pitched, and a party of boys on one part, and a party of gentlemen in another, were playing cricket. Beyond this was a large meadow with rich groups of trees under which a flock of sheep were reposing, and girls and women with children were playing. While watching the cricketers we were threatened with a shower, and hastened back to look for shelter, which we found in a pagoda on an island approached by a Chinese bridge. It was soon filled, as were the other ornamental buildings, by a crowd of those, who, like ourselves, had been overtaken in the grounds by the rain, and I was glad to observe that the privileges of the garden were enjoyed equally by all classes. The site of the garden was, ten years ago, a flat sterile clay farm. It was placed in the hands of Mr Paxton in June 1844, by whom it was laid out in its present form by June the following year.

FREDERICK OLMSTEAD

AND CENTRAL PARK

It is one great purpose of the Park to supply to the hundreds of thousands of tired workers, who have no opportunity to spend their summers in the country, a specimen of God's handiwork that shall be to them inexpensively, what a month or two in The White Mountains or the Adirondacks is, at great cost, to those in easier circumstances.

FREDERICK OLMSTEAD

AMERICAN ESTATES

The embellishment of nature, which we call Landscape Gardening, springs naturally from a love of country life, an attachment to a certain spot, and a desire to render that place attractive—a feeling which seems more or less strongly fixed in the minds of all men. But we should convey a false impression, were we to state that it may be applied with equal success to residences of every class and size, in the country. Lawn and trees, being its two essential elements, some of the beauties of Landscape Gardening may, indeed, be shown wherever a wood or grass surface and half-a-dozen trees are within our reach; we may even with such scanty space, have tasteful grouping, varied surface, and agreeably curved walks; but our art, to appear to advantage, requires some extent of surface—its lines should lose themselves indefinitely, and unite agreeably and gradually with those of the surrounding country.

In the case of large landed estates, its capabilities may be displayed to their full extent, as from fifty to five hundred acres may be devoted to a park or pleasure grounds. Most of its beauty and all its charms, may, however, be enjoyed in ten or twenty acres, fortunately situated, and well treated; and Landscape Gardening, in America, combined and working in harmony as it is with our fine scenery, is already beginning to give us results scarcely less beautiful than those produced by its finest effects abroad. The lovely villa residences of our noble river and lake margins, when well treated—even in a few acres of tasteful foreground—seem so entirely to appropriate the whole adjacent landscape, and to mingle so sweetly in their outlines with the woods, the valleys and the shores around them, that the effects are often truly enchanting.

ANDREW JACKSON DOWNING

SWANN'S WAY

One day my grandfather said to my father: "Don't you remember Swann's telling us yesterday that his wife and daughter had gone off to Rheims and that he was taking the opportunity of spending a day or two in Paris? We might go along by the park, since the ladies are not at home; that will make it a little shorter."

We stopped for a moment by the fence. Lilac-time was nearly over; some of the trees still thrust aloft, in tall purple chandeliers, their tiny balls of blossom, but in many places among their foliage where, only a week before, they had still been breaking in waves of fragrant foam, these were now spent and shrivelled and discoloured, a hollow scum, dry and scentless. My grandfather pointed out to my father in what respects the appearance of the place was still the same, and how far it had altered since the walk that he had taken with old M.

Swann, on the day of his wife's death; and he seized the opportunity to tell us, once again, the story of that walk.

In front of us a path bordered with nasturtiums rose in the full glare of the sun towards the house. But to our right the park stretched away in the distance, on level ground. Overshadowed by the tall trees which stood close around it, an 'ornamental water' had been constructed by Swann's parents but, even in his most artificial creations, nature is the material upon which man has to work; certain spots will persist in remaining surrounded by the vassals of their own especial sovereignty, and will raise their immemorial standards among all the 'laid-out' scenery of a park, just as they would have done far from any human interference, in a solitude which must everywhere return to engulf them, springing up out of the necessities of their exposed position, and superimposing itself upon the work of man's hands. And so it was that, at the foot of the path which led down to this artificial lake, there might be seen, in its two tiers woven of trailing forget-me-nots below and of periwinkle flowers above, the natural, delicate, blue garland which binds the luminous, shadowed brows of water-nymphs; while the iris, its swords sweeping every way in regal profusion, stretched out over agrimony and water-growing king-cups the lilied sceptres, tattered glories of yellow and purple, of the kingdom of the lake.

MARCEL PROUST

A PLEASURE GARDEN

Image to yourself, my dear Letty, a spacious garden, part laid out in delightful walks, bounded with high hedges and trees, and paved with gravel; part exhibiting a wonderful assemblage of the most picturesque and striking objects, pavilions, lodges, groves, grottoes, lawns, temples, and cascades; porticoes, colonades, and rotundos; adorned with pillars, statues, and painting; the whole illuminated with an infinite number of lamps, disposed in different figures of suns, stars, and constellations; the place crowded with the gayest company, ranging through those blissful shades, or supping in different lodges on cold collations, enlivened with mirth, freedom, and good humour, and animated by an excellent band of music. Among the vocal performers I had the happiness to hear the celebrated Mrs —, whose voice was loud and so shrill that it made my head ache through excess of pleasure.

TOBIAS SMOLLETT

PARKS AND ESTATES

By the cunning use of perspective tricks, the eye can be deceived into believing that a tiny garden is much larger, but attempts at the reverse, to miniaturize extensive landscapes, are rarely successful. The parks of great estates often depend for their best effects on the fact that the landscaper's patron owned most of the horizon. Frequently they could remove mature trees from distant hedges to create 'Windows' to attractive features even further away. And it is seldom possible to make an average large garden of an acre or two appear so limitless. So that without control over several miles of territory it is probably better to create a personal horizon on the limits of your own land. While this 'fortress garden' approach might seem limiting at least it ensures that having created a satisfying vista the effect isn't ruined when someone else puts up a monstrous building which compels attention no matter where you sit.

If your own high screen of trees is to be effective it will inevitably make the boundaries of your garden obvious. This in its turn would make any attempt at a grandiose treatment of the enclosed land seem absurd. Faced with the problem of creating a new garden in these circumstances it is better to abandon any notions of establishing avenues of tall trees culminating in large ornamental features. To fit them on to the plot the avenues would have to be indecently narrow and any of their essential sense of grandeur would vanish. New gardeners under these circumstances would be wiser to opt for something less ambitious – an interestingly designed area close to the house with a wild garden beyond, perhaps.

G.R.

Herbal and
Botanic Gardens

PHYSICK GARDEN

Amongst ye severall famous structures & curiosities wherewith ye flourishing University of Oxford is enriched, that of ye Publick Physick Garden deserves not ye last place, being a matter of great use & ornament, prouving serviceable not only to all Physitians, Apothecaryes, and those who are more imediately concerned in the practise of Physick, but to persons of all qualities serving to help ye diseased and for ye delight & pleasure of those of perfect health, containing therein 3000 severall sorts of plants for ye honor of our nation and Universitie & service of ye Commonwealth . . . Old Jacob Bobart father to this present Jacob may be said to be ye man yt first gave life & beauty to this famous place, who by his care & industry replenish'd the walls, wth all manner of good fruits our clime would ripen, & bedeck the earth wth great variety of trees plants & exotic flowers, dayly augmented by the Botanists, who bring them hither from ye remote Quarters of ye world . . .

Here I may take leave to speak a word or two of old Jacob who is now fled from his Earthly Paradise. As to Country he was by birth a German born in Brunswick that great Rum-Brewhouse of Europe: In his younger dayes as I remember I have heard him say he was sometime a Soldier by which Imploy and travail he had opportunitie of Augmenting his knowledge, for to his native Dutch he added the English Language, and he did understand Latine pretty well. As to fabrick of body he was by nature very well built, (his son in respect of him but a shrimp) tall straite and strong with square shoulders and a head well set upon them. In his latter days he delighted to weare a long Beard and once against Whitsontide had a fancy to tagg it with silver, which drew much Company in the Physick Garden.

THOMAS BASKERVILLE

POIGNANT HEARBES

That quarter of the Garden which serveth our house with poignant hearbes instead of sauce, to give a commendable tast and seasoning to our meat, sheweth plainly that the master and mistresse thereof were not woont to run in the Merchants' bookes for Spicerie, but chaunged the Grocer or Apothecaries' shop, for the Garden ... And as for the other quarters set out with beds of floures and sweet smelling hearbes, what reckoning was made of them in old time may appeare by this, that a man could not heretofore come by a commoner's house within the citie, but he should see the windowes beautified with greene quishins wrought and tapissed with floures of all colours, resembling daily to their view the Gardens indeed which were in out-villages, as being in the very heart of the citie, they might think themselves in the countrey.

PLINY

MANY SORTS OF HERBES

... First, to begin with that which hath beene most anciently received, which is Thrift. This is an everliving greene herbe, which many take to border their beds, and set their knots and trayles, and therein much delight, because it will grow thicke and bushie, and may be kept, being cut with a paire of Garden sheares, in some good handsome manner and proportion for a time, and besides, in the Summer time send forth many short stalkes of pleasant flowers, to decke up an house among other sweet herbes.

... Germander is another herbe, in former times also much used, and yet also in many places; and because it will growe thicke, and may be kept also in some forme and proportion with cutting, and that the cuttings are much used as a strawing herbe for houses, being pretty and sweet, is also much affected by divers ...

Hyssope hath also been used to be set about a knot, and, being sweet, will serve for strewings, as Germander.

... Marierome, Savorie, and Thyme, in the like manner being sweet herbes, are used to border up beds and knots.

... Lavander Cotton also, being finely slipped and set, is of many, and those of the highest respect of late daies, accepted, both for the beauty and forme of the herbe, being of a whitish greene mealy colour, for his sent smelling somewhat strong, being everliving and abiding greene all the Winter, will, by cutting, be kept in as even proportion as any other herbe may be.

... The rarity & novelty of this herbe, being for the most part but in the Gardens of great persons, doth cause it to be of the highest regard; it must therefore be renewed wholly every second or third yeare at the most, because of the great growing thereof. Slips of Juniper or Yew are also received of some & planted, because they are alwayes greene, and that the Juniper especially hath not that ill sent that Boxe hath.

... To border the whole square or knot about, to serve

as a hedge thereunto, every one taketh what likest him best; as either Privet alone, or sweet Bryer, and white Thorne enterlaced together, and Roses of one, or two, or more sorts placed here and there amongst them. Some also take Lavender, Rosemary, Sage, Southernwood, Lavander Cotton, or some such other thing. Some againe plant Cornell Trees, and plash them, or keepe them lowe, to forme them into a hedge. And some againe take a lowe prickly shrubbe, that abideth alwayes greene, called in Latine Pyracantha, which in time will make an ever greene hedge or border, and when it beareth fruit, which are like unto Hawthorne berries, make a glorious shew among the greene leaves in the Winter time, when no other shrubbes have fruit or flowers.

JOHN PARKINSON

HERB GARDENS

Despite the blandishments of partisans of the organic approach to everything, few gardeners will seriously grow herbs with the intention of using them as medicine. But while they have been superseded by products of the pharmaceutical industry in the bathroom chest, they daily become more important as aids to more ambitious cooking.

As more and more shoppers strive to protect their families from the synthetic by buying fresh or cool chain produce for processing in the kitchen, their need for the greater variety of fresh herbs demanded by adventurous dishes increases. In the recent past a few pots of commonplace herbs like mint and parsley kept on the windowsill or outside the kitchen door sufficed. Today something much more suitable is required.

Several attractive formulae have been tried; most of them exploit the fact that many herbs are beautiful, decorative plants in their own right and merit beds of their own. Two approaches which have proved very satisfactory are the herb pavement and the herb clock.

The pavement is a terraced area near the kitchen generally clad with small (one-foot-square is ideal) paving slabs. In places, one or more slabs are omitted so that herbs can be planted in the soil underlay which remains exposed. A single one-foot-square area provides sufficient of the compact herbs which are required only in small quantities. Several one-foot-square areas might be needed for the herbs in high demand, or those, like the large sages or fennel, which demand more space.

Keen herb growers adopting this approach use their own aesthetic judgement when it comes to mixing herbs of several types in a single planted area. They give the placement of individual plants as much thought as they would if they were composing a normal herbaceous border.

The herbal clock was a very attractive feature in many Victorian gardens. It consists of a circular bed some six to eight feet in diameter surrounded by a firm path, usually paved or gravelled, or best of all topped with patterned old brick. A fountain, figure, vase or some other ornament is usually set on a small podium (one foot diameter) at the centre of the bed. Narrow edging slabs or bricks radiating from the centre of the circle divide it into twelve or more separate beds into which individual herbs can be planted. Several particular herbs can be planted in a single bed with the tallest stationed near the centre of the circle.

G.R.

Town Gardens

DAINTIE PLACES IN THE CITIE

And even in these our daies, under the name of Gardens and Hortyards, there goe many daintie places of pleasure within the very citie; and under the colour also and title of them men are possessed of faire closes and pleasant fields, yea, and of proper houses with a good circuit of ground lying to them, like pretie fermes and graunges in the countrey; all of which they tearme by the name of Gardens.

PLINY THE ELDER

LETTER TO MR NICHOLLS

Pembroke College, June 24, 1769

And so you have a garden of your own, and you plant and transplant, and are very dirty and amused! Are you not ashamed of yourself? Why, I have no such thing, you monster, nor ever shall be either dirty or amused as long as I live. My gardens are in the window like those of a lodger up three pairs of stairs in Petticoat-lane, or Camomile-street, and they go to bed regularly under the same roof that I do. Dear, how charming it must be to walk out in one's own *garding*, and sit on a bench in the open air, with a fountain and leaden statue, and a rolling stone, and an arbour: have a care of sore throats though, and the *ague*.

THOMAS GRAY

FROM HIS PRISON

But I possessed another surprise; which was a garden.
There was a little yard outside the room, railed off from
another belonging to the neighbouring ward. This yard
I shut in with green palings, adorned it with a trellis,
bordered it with a thick bed of earth from a nursery, and
even contrived to have a grass-plot. The earth I filled
with flowers and young trees. There was an apple-tree,
from which we managed to get a pudding the second
year. As to my flowers, they were allowed to be perfect.
Thomas Moore, who came to see me with Lord Byron,
told me he had seen no such heart's-ease. I bought the
Parnaso Italiano while in prison, and used often to think
of a passage in it, while looking at this miniature piece of
horticulture:—

Mio picciol orto,
A me sei vigna, e campo, e selva, e prato.—Baldi.

My little garden,
To me thou'rt vineyard, field, and meadow, and wood.

Here I wrote and read in fine weather, sometimes
under an awning. In autumn, my trellises were hung
with scarlet-runners, which added to the flowery
investment. I used to shut my eyes in my arm-chair, and
affect to think myself hundreds of miles off.

But my triumph was in issuing forth of a morning. A
wicket out of the garden led into the large one belonging
to the prison. The latter was only for vegetables; but it
contained a cherry tree, which I saw twice in blossom. I
parcelled out the ground in my imagination into
favourite districts. I made a point of dressing myself as if

for a long walk; and then, putting on my gloves, and taking my book under my arm, stepped forth, requesting my wife not to wait dinner if I was too late.

LEIGH HUNT

A JAPANESE TOWN GARDEN

This is commonly square, with a back door, and wall'd in very neatly, like a cistern, or pond, for which reason it is call'd Tsubo, which in the Japanese language signifies a large water-trough or cistern. There are few good houses and Inns, but what have their Tsubo. If there not be room enough for a garden, they have at least an old ingrafted plum, cherry, or apricock tree. The older, the more crooked and monstrous the tree is, the greater value they put upon it. Sometimes they let the branches grow into the rooms. In order to make it bear larger flowers, and in greater quantity, they commonly cut it to a few, perhaps two or three branches. It cannot be denied, that the great number of beautiful, incarnate, and double flowers, which they bear in the proper Season, are a surprizingly curious ornament to this back part of the house, but they have this disadvantage, that they bear no fruit. In some small houses, and Inns of less note, where there is not room enough, neither for a garden, nor trees, they have at least an opening or window to let the light fall into the back rooms, before which, for the amusement and diversion of travellers, is put a small tub, full of water, wherein they commonly keep some gold or silver fish, as they call them, being fish with gold or silver-colour'd Tails alive. For a farther ornament of the same place, there is generally a flower-pot or two standing there. Sometimes they plant some dwarf-trees there, which will grow easily upon pumice, or other porous stones, without any ground at all, provided the root be put into the water, from whence it will suck up sufficient nourishment. Ordinary people often plant the same kind of trees before the street-doors, for their diversion, as well as for an ornament to their houses.

ENGELBERT KAEMPFER

TOWN GARDENS

The most successful town gardeners are those who accept their urban situation. Realizing that buildings, frequently of a rather formal style, are always going to dominate, they shun the idea that their garden should in any way attempt to be cottagey. They don't try to delude us that their plot forms part of a hamlet in some remote corner of the elysian fields.

They tend to be very selective and niggardly about the plants which they use. They choose a few bold plants with strong architectural characteristics planted rather formally, which will read well against masonry, softening as well as being harmonious with it, rather than trying to dominate the buildings with the sort of anarchic riot of vegetation which often looks so well in a rural setting.

Pure stage-craft plays a much more important role in town gardening than it does in the country. And features like very formal high-quality paving, raked gravel surfaces, plants in troughs and vases, espaliered *Magnolia grandiflora* or figs on walls, should be used as a setting for the house.

Good town gardeners often choose ornamental rather than herbaceous ways of making their homes more attractive. They use well-proportioned formal trelliage designs to relieve the monotony of walls rather than festooning them with climbing plants.

Where town houses front directly on to a street visual relief is best provided by window boxes.

But good town gardeners will be satisfied with a permanent planting of attractive evergreens in their boxes, as a background for a few bright small flowering plants introduced as they become available on market stalls, rather than trying to use them as fully productive market gardens by cramming them with lettuces and tomatoes.

G.R.

A Child's Garden

LITTLE BEDS

The garden was a wide enclosure, surrounded with walls so high as to exclude every glimpse of prospect; a covered verandah ran down one side, and broad walks bordered a middle space divided into scores of little beds: these beds were assigned as gardens for the pupils to cultivate, and each bed had an owner. When full of flowers they would doubtless look pretty.

CHARLOTTE BRONTË

THE MOLE'S GARDEN

The Mole struck a match, and by its light the Rat saw that they were standing in an open space, neatly swept and sanded underfoot, and directly facing them was Mole's little front door, with 'Mole End' painted, in Gothic lettering, over the bell-pull at the side.

Mole reached down a lantern from a nail on the wall and lit it, and the Rat, looking round him, saw that they were in a sort of fore-court. A garden seat stood on one side of the door, and on the other, a roller; for the Mole, who was a tidy animal when at home, could not stand having his ground kicked up by other animals into little runs that ended in earth-heaps. On the walls hung wire baskets with ferns in them, alternating with brackets carrying plaster statuary – Garibaldi, and the infant Samuel, and Queen Victoria, and other heroes of modern Italy. Down one side of the fore-court ran a skittle alley, with benches along it and little wooden tables marked with rings that hinted at beer-mugs. In the middle was a small round pond containing goldfish and surrounded by a cockle-shell border. Out of the centre of the pond rose a fanciful erection clothed in more cockle-shells and topped off by a large silvered glass ball that reflected everything all wrong and had a very pleasing effect.

KENNETH GRAHAME

PLACES OF MY INFANCY

But for a child the garden was brim full of surprises. In a corner was a big thicket filled with cacti and rare shrubs, the kingdom of Nino, head gardener and my great friend, he too redhaired like so many at Santa Margherita, perhaps derived from the Norman Filangeri. There was a bamboo thicket, growing thick and sturdy around a secondary fountain, in the shade of which was an open space for games, with a swing from which long before my time Pietro Scalea, later Minister of War, fell and broke his arm. In one of the side alleys, embedded in the wall, was a big cage destined at one time for monkeys, in which a girl cousin and I shut ourselves one day, a Sunday morning when the garden was open to the townsfolk who stopped in mute amazement to gaze, uncertainly, at these dressed-up simians. There was a 'dolls' house', built for the diversion of my mother and her four sisters, made of red brick, with window frames in *pietra serena*; now, with its roof and floors fallen in, it was the only disconsolate corner of the big garden, the remainder of which Nino kept in admirable order with every tree well pruned, every alley yellow-pebbled, every bush clipped.

GIUSEPPE DI LAMPEDUSA

DOLL'S GARDEN

The doll's house (the door of which occupied the whole frontage, the architect having forgotten the stairs) stood centrally at the upper end of our domain, representing the family mansion; 'the gardener', a tin soldier in full uniform with fixed bayonet, spent most of his time lying on his stomach, his form being fragile and the situation windy; and the fishponds were triumphs of engineering skill. Mine was a metal pan, which had formerly been used for culinary purposes, placed in an excavation prepared for it, and containing a real fish, about the size of a whitebait, and caught by hand in the brook hard by. One of my sisters produced, I must confess, a more brilliant effect with some bits of looking-glass, but they lacked the gracefulness of nature and the charm of reality . . .

The conservatory was a noble construction adjoining the family mansion, but of larger dimensions – a square hand-glass, which looked as though it had been in a phenomenal hail-storm, and had only one qualification for plant culture, a free circulation of air.

I dwell upon these adjuncts to horticulture rather than upon the produce of the soil, because in the latter department we did not attain a like success. We were not on the best of terms with our gardener – the real gardener, not the tin soldier – and he would not help us. Our ways (over the flower-beds) were not his ways, and he objected to the promiscuous use of his syringe and the premature removal of his fruit. We differed, again, on the subject of transplanting. It seemed to us an easier and more satisfactory process to transfer specimens in full beauty from his garden to our own, rather than to watch their tardy growth and tedious afflorescence.

Unhappily for us, the specimens did not seem to like it.

SAMUEL REYNOLDS HOLE

OUR LITTLE GARDENS

The stonecrop that on ruins comes
 And hangs like golden balls—
How oft to reach its shining blooms
 We scaled the mossy walls!
And weeds—we gathered weeds as well,
 Of all that bore a flower,
And tied our little posies up
 Beneath the eldern bower.

Our little gardens there we made
 Of blossoms all arow,
And though they had no roots at all
 We hoped to see them grow;
And in the cart rut after showers
 Of sudden summer rain
We filled our tiny waterpots
 And cherished them in vain.

JOHN CLARE

MUHAMMAD DIN'S GARDEN

He had half buried the polo-ball in dust, and stuck six
shrivelled old marigold flowers in a circle round it.
Outside that circle again was a rude square, traced out
in bits of red brick alternating with fragments of broken
china; the whole bonded by a little bank of dust . . . it
was only the play of a baby and did not much disfigure

my garden . . . always fashioning magnificent palaces from stale flowers thrown away by the bearer, smooth water-worn pebbles, bits of broken glass, and feathers pulled, I fancy, from my fowls.

RUDYARD KIPLING

LITTLE WOMEN

The garden had to be put in order, and each sister had a quarter of the little plot to do what she liked with . . . for the girls' tastes differed as much as their characters. Meg had roses and heliotrope, myrtle and a little orange tree in it. Jo's bed was never alike two seasons, for she was always trying experiments. This year it was to be a plantation of sunflowers . . . Beth had old-fashioned, fragrant flowers in her garden – sweet peas and mignonette, larkspur, pinks, pansies, and southern-wood, with chickweed for the birds and catnip for the pussies. Amy had a bower in hers, rather small and earwiggy, but very pretty to look at, with honeysuckles and morning glories hanging their coloured horns and bells in graceful wreaths all over it; tall white lilies, delicate ferns and as many brilliant, picturesque plants as would consent to blossom there.

LOUISA M. ALCOTT

THE CHILD'S APPLE TREE

It was a marvel how soundly the tree slept: so cold and drawn in upon itself, as if it were dead. It was the boy's favourite tree: his own, given him by his father. He smoothed his fingers along the wrinkles of its skin, and nuzzled it with his cheek. It had yielded its first fruit in the year that he was born.

William loved everything about the garden, even in the winter when the vegetables dissolved in long green smears and melted into the earth. Only a few scrawny cabbages, tall and thin, with woody stalks like saplings, had withstood the bite of the frost. Their hard veiny leaves had repelled every attack by beak and claw, and the fire would need many armfuls of wood to boil them into soup. William knew every tree in the garden: the plums and the pears, the nuts, the apples and the medlars. He understood their every phase and mood; could feel in the air the first faint whispers of seasonal change that would bring new leaf, or the unfolding of blossom, or the sweet mellowing of fruit. But to his own tree he was more even than a friend: a brother. Since their first shared year of life, thirteen years ago, there had been two sisters borne to William's family, and every autumn the brimming basketfuls of fruit. Each apple was brushed with crimson where it faced the sun, and each grew exactly to the size of William's palm.

RICHARD GIRLING

CHILDREN'S GARDENS

Most parents fail dismally in their efforts to create gardens with the requirements of children in mind. Unless the garden is very large, areas designated exclusively for children's use – skid pans for trikes, swings and roundabouts, sandpits, mini-football and cricket pitches etc – quickly become grass-less and grace-less and ruin any attempt at pleasing garden design. And what is saddest is that unless the family is of Victorian proportions they so quickly become redundant. No potential winner of a grand prix or the Tour de France, no budding international left-half or hooker, no flashing future middle-order batsman or Wimbledon star will be satisfied with the restricted facilities which even the most indulgent parents can provide at home. So the best advice to parent gardeners wishing to satisfy their children's needs is DON'T TRY – you will be wasting your time and making your garden resemble Bedlam.

It is also a fact that while a tiny minority of children are of such a curious and contemplative nature that they will become absorbed by serious gardening from the moment that they are strong enough to turn soil with a handfork, most of them aren't. Gardening yields its rewards far too slowly for impatient youngsters. One glance into their bedroom would tell you that they are likely to obtain scant satisfaction from a tidy and weedfree bed.

But, in order to salve their consciences about 'bringing up the child to have a reverence for nature' parents ought to consider seriously devoting an out-of-the-way square yard of the vegetable plot or border for a little 'garden of their own'. In fact the managers of the Lowwood Orphanage described by Charlotte Brontë, in the first quote in the preceding section, had it just about right.

G.R.

Birds

PEACOCKS FOR ZULEIKA DOBSON

Luncheon passed in almost unbroken silence. Both Zuleika and the Duke were ravenously hungry, as people always are after the stress of any great emotional crisis. Between them, they made very short work of a cold chicken, a salad, a gooseberry-tart and a Camembert. The Duke filled his glass again and again. The cold classicism of his face had been routed by the new romantic movement which had swept over his soul. He looked two or three months older than when first I showed him to my reader.

He drank his coffee at one draught, pushed back his chair, threw away the cigarette he had just lit. "Listen!" he said.

Zuleika folded her hands on her lap.

"You do not love me. I accept as final your hint that you never will love me. I need not say—could not, indeed, ever say—how deeply, deeply you have pained me. As lover, I am rejected. But that rejection," he continued, striking the table, "is no stopper to my suit. It does but drive me to the use of arguments . . . You, Miss Dobson, what are you? A conjurer, and a vagrant; without means, save such as you can earn by the sleight of your hand; without position; without a home; all unguarded but by your own self-respect. That you follow an honourable calling, I do not for one moment deny. I do, however, ask you to consider how great are its perils and hardships, its fatigues and inconveniences. From all these evils I offer you instant refuge. I offer you, Miss Dobson, a refuge more glorious and more augustly gilded than you, in your airiest flights of fancy, can ever have hoped for or imagined. I own about 340,000 acres. My town residence is in St. James's

Square. Tankerton, of which you may have seen photographs, is the chief of my country seats. It is a Tudor house, set on the ridge of a valley. The valley, its park, is halved by a stream so narrow that the deer leap across. The gardens are estraded upon the slope. Round the house runs a wide paven terrace. There are always two or three peacocks trailing their sheathed feathers along the balustrade, and stepping how stiffly! as though they had just been unharnessed from Juno's chariot. Two flights of shallow steps lead down to the flowers and fountains. Oh, the gardens are wonderful. There is a Jacobean garden of white roses. Between the ends of two pleached alleys, under a dome of branches, is a little lake, with a Triton of black marble, and with water-lilies. Hither and thither under the archipelago of water-lilies, dart gold-fish – tongues of flame in the dark water. There is also a long strait alley of clipped yew. It ends in an alcove for a pagoda of painted porcelain which the Prince Regent—peace be to his ashes!— presented to my great-grandfather. There are many twisting paths, and sudden aspects, and devious, fantastic arbours. Are you fond of horses? In my stables of pinewood and plated-silver seventy are installed. Not all of them together could vie in power with one of the meanest of my motor-cars."

MAX BEERBOHM

INNUMERABLE FLIGHTS OF BRIGHT GREEN PARROTS

Come to the Taj Mahal; descriptions of this wonderfully lovely place are simply silly, as no words can describe it at all. What a garden! What flowers! What gorgeously dressed and be-ringed women; some of them very good-looking too, and all well clothed though apparently poor. Men, mostly in white, some with red shawls, some quite dressed in red, or red-brown; orange, yellow, scarlet, or purple shawls, or white; effects of colour absolutely astonishing, the great centre of the picture being ever the vast glittering ivory-white Taj Mahal, and the accompaniment and contrast of the dark green of cypresses with the rich yellow-green trees of all sorts! And then the effect of the innumerable flights of bright green parrots flitting across like live emeralds; and of the scarlet poinciannas and countless other flowers beaming bright off the dark green! The tinker or tinpot bird ever at work; pigeons, hoopoes, and I think a new sort of mynah, pale dove colour and gray; also squirrels, and all tame, and endlessly numerous. Poinsettias are in huge crimson masses, and the purple flowered bougainvillaea runs up the cypress trees. Aloes also, and some new sort of fern or palm, I don't know which. Below the Taj Mahal is a scene of pilgrim-washing and shrines, altogether Indian and lovely.

What can I do here? Certainly not the architecture, which I naturally shall not attempt, except perhaps in a slight sketch of one or two direct garden views. Henceforth, let the inhabitants of the world be divided into two classes—them as has seen the Taj Mahal; and them as hasn't.

EDWARD LEAR

GO CHIRPE

Sweet birds, that sit and sing amid the shadie valleys,
And see how sweetly Phillis walks amid her garden
    alleys,

Go round about her bower, and sing as ye are bidden:
To her is only knowne his faith that from the world is
    hidden.
And she among you all that hath the sweetest voice,
Go chirpe of him that never told, yet never chang'd, his
    choice.

NICHOLAS BRETON

BIRDS AND THE PHOENIX

The clouds began to clear, the mist rarified;
    In an herber I saw, brought where I was,
There birds on the briar sang on every side;
    With alleys ensanded about in compass,
    The banks enturfèd with singular solas,
Enrailèd with rosers, and vines engrapèd;
It was a new comfort of sorrowis escapèd.

In the midst of a conduit, that curiously was cast,
    With pipes of gold, engushing out streams;
Of crystal the clearness these waters far past,
    Enswimming with roaches, barbellis and
        breams,
    Whose scales ensilvered against the sun-beams
Englistered, that joyous it was to behold.
Then furthermore about me my sight I revol'd,

Where I saw growing a goodly laurel tree,
    Enverdurèd with leaves continually green;
Above in the top a bird of Araby
    Men call a phoenix, her wings between
    She beat up a fire with the sparks full keen;

With branches and boughes of the sweet olive,
Whose fragrant flower was chief preservative.

JOHN SKELTON

FROM "THE KINGIS QUAIR"

Now was there maid, fast by the towris wall,
   A gardin faire, and in the corneris set
Ane herbere grene: with wandis long and small
   Railit about; and so with treis set
   Was all the place, and hawthorn hegis knet,
That lif was none walking there forby,
That might within scarse ony wight aspye.

So thik the bewis and the leves grene
   Beschadit all the aleyes that there were,
And middis every herbere might be sene
   That scharpe grene swete jenepere,
   Growing so faire with branchis here and there,
That, as it semit to a lif without,
The bewis spred the herbere all about;

And on the smalle grene twistis sat
   The litill swete nightingale, and song
So loud and clere the ympnis consecrat
   Of lufis use, now soft, now loud among,
   That all the garding and the wallis rong
Right of their song . . .

KING JAMES I OF SCOTLAND

FROM "THE ROMAUNT OF
THE ROSE"

And forth, withoute wordis mo,
In at the wiket went I thro,
That Ydelnesse hadde opened me,
Into that gardyn fair to see.
    And whan I was inne, iwys,
Myn herte was ful glad of this,
For wel wende I ful sikerly
Have been in paradys erthly,
So fair it was that, trusteth wel,
It semede a place espirituel.
For certys, as at my devys,
Ther is no place in paradys
So good inne for to dwelle or be
As in that gardyn, thoughte me.
For ther was many a bridd syngyng,
Thoroughout the yerd al thringyng;
In many places were nyghtyngales,
Alpes, fynches, and wodewales,
That in her swete song deliten
In thilke places as they habiten.
There myghte men see many flokkes
Of turtles and laverokes.
Chalaundres fele sawe I there,
That wery, nygh forsongen were;
And thrustles, terins, and mavys,
That songen for to wynne hem prys,
And eke to sormounte in her song
That other briddes hem among.
By note made fair servyse
These briddes, that I you devyse;
They songe her song as faire and wel

As angels don espirituel.
And trusteth wel, whan I hem herde,
Ful lustily and wel I ferde;
For never yitt such melodye
Was herd of man that myghte dye.

(TRANSLATED BY) GEOFFREY CHAUCER

GIVE BIRDS MORE SCOPE

For aviaries, I like them not, except they be of that
largeness as they may be turfed, and have living plants
and bushes set in them; that the birds may have more
scope and natural nestling, and that no foulness appear
in the floor of the aviary. So I have made a platform of a
princely garden, partly by precept, partly by drawing,
not a model, but some general lines of it; and in this I
have spared no cost.

FRANCIS BACON

IN ISLAM – THE NIGHTINGALE

Mazanderan is the bower of spring,
Tulips and hyacinths abound
On every lawn; and all around
Blooms like a garden in its prime,
Fostered by that delicious clime,
The nightingale sits on every spray
And pours his soft melodious lay;
Each rural spot its sweets discloses,
Each streamlet is the dew of roses.

FIRDAWSI

A CONSORT OF BIRDS

It is a pleasure to the Eare to heare the sweet notes and
tunes of singing Birds, whose company a man shall be
sure to have in an Orchard, which is more pleasant
there, than elsewhere, because of other concurrent
pleasures there; a Consort of Musicke is more pleasant
than a single Instrument.

RALPH AUSTEN

A CHIEF GRACE

One chief grace that adornes an Orchard I cannot let
slippe. A broode of Nightingales, who with their several
notes and tunes, with a strong delightsome voyce, out of
a weake body, will beare you company night and day.
She loves (and lives in) bots of wood in her heart. She
will help you to cleanse your trees of Caterpillars, and
all noysome wormes and flyes.

Neither will the Silly Wren be behind in Summer,
with her distinct whistle (like a sweet Recorder) to
cheere your spirits.

The Black-bird and Threstle (for I take it the
Thrush sings not, but devours) sing loudly in a May
morning, and delight the Eare much (and you neede not
want their company, if you have ripe Cherryes or
Berries, and would as gladly as the rest doe you
pleasure): But I had rather want their company than my
fruit.

What shall I say? 1000 of delights are in an
Orchard: and sooner shall I be weary, then I can reckon
the least part of that pleasure, which one, that hath and
loves an Orchard, may finde therein.

WILLIAM LAWSON

BIRDS LIKE A CHOIR

The garden, it was long and wide
And filled with great unconscious peace;
All the old trees were tall and large,
And all the birds –

The birds, he said, were like a choir
Of lively boys,
Who never went to school,
But sang instead.

He told me of the trailing flowers
Hung on the ruined walls;
The rivers and their waterfalls;
The hidden woods; the lawns; the bowers.
Small cool plantations; palm and vine,
With fig-tree growing by their side,
And violet and maidenhair.

HAROLD MUNRO

BIRDS

The strident squawk of peacocks is a common sound in great gardens like the one the Duke described to Zuleika. But ornamental birds are rare in private gardens. However, if gardeners are prepared to become involved in a demanding feeding routine and can improvise suitable sleeping quarters, there seem to be few limits to the type of birds whose bright plumage will supplement flowers as providers of colour in the garden.

Emerald and gold parrots, grey West African cranes, pink flamingoes and shiny black East Indies ducks – among many others – will parade on lawns and among borders without doing any damage if they are chosen and tended carefully. They become centres of bright animation on dull days or when the garden is suffering a summer dead period.

If a reasonable-sized pond is available, a good 'starter kit' would be a pair of Mandarin or Carolina ducks. A barrel with a hole in the end, raised off the ground on its side, with a timber access ramp near the water's edge, will make an ideal home. A daily bowl of wheat mixed with poultry pellets will leave them little appetite for garden plants.

But, be warned, geese must be avoided at all costs because they will wreck everything which they can reach! And unless the birds are pinioned they will fly away.

G.R.

Index